THE HISTORY OF
THE YORKSHIRE MUSEUM

Front Cover: An early view of the Museum. Date and artist unknown.
Reproduced from a copper plate in the Yorkshire Museum archives.

THE HISTORY OF
THE YORKSHIRE MUSEUM
and its geological collections

by

Barbara J. Pyrah

William Sessions Limited
York, England

ISBN 1 85072 042 8 Paperback

Printed in 10 on 11 point Plantin Typeface
by William Sessions Limited
The Ebor Press
York, England

Contents

Illustrations

Introduction

THE YORKSHIRE PHILOSOPHICAL SOCIETY was one of the earliest provincial societies devoted entirely to philosophical, as opposed to literary, studies. Founded in York in 1822, in a city which even today remembers its mediaeval role as the second city of England, the Society built up one of the largest geological collections in the provinces, together with collections of archaeology, natural history, ethnology, numismatics and the decorative arts.

Once the initial enthusiastic years were past, the maintenance of the Museum became a minority interest within the membership, most of whom were motivated to join the Society by the provision of lecture courses, or by the facilities offered in the Museum Gardens. However, there always was a strong 'inner circle' of members who were deeply committed to the future of the Museum, although much of their field research was carried out within associated societies and clubs rather than within the Y.P.S. itself, and the well-being of the Museum remained one of the central concerns of the Society, even after the Museum passed into local government ownership in 1961.

The three major divisions of subject within the Museum – geology, archaeology and natural history – were present almost from the beginning, the existence of geology as a subject separate from natural history being due to the special circumstances of the foundation of the Society.

The fortunes of the various departments were influenced by factors such as local discoveries and the interests of individual members. The one common factor for much of the time was lack of space within the Museum, this led to crowded galleries and storage areas, with consequent friction between individual Curators. Financial stringencies restricted expansion of the building, but had only a minor impact on the activities of individual departments, as Honorary Curators not only gave of their time, but also provided much of the money needed to buy materials for labelling, conservation and storage of specimens under their care.

1

While the archaeology and natural history departments were soundly based on readily available local material and local field groups, which brought to the Museum active workers with a wide range of interests, geology was supported by only a small band of workers. Thus, after the first few years, the geology department had only one Honorary Curator, while other departments sometimes had several, covering different aspects of the subject between them. During the 19th century the balance was maintained between geology and the other departments because the professional Keeper of the Museum was a geologist, although his duties always covered the whole range of the Museum's collections. When in the 20th century this tradition was broken growth of the geological collections virtually ceased.

These differences between the departments are reflected within the collections. The archaeological and biological collections contain a wealth of specimens from sites in York and its immediate surroundings, while specimens from outside the county make up only a small proportion of the material.

The geological collections are in complete contrast. Material from York and its immediate surroundings is restricted to a few Pleistocene bones and glacial erratics. There is an important collection of material from the further reaches of the county, in particular the Yorkshire Dales and the Yorkshire Coast, but the main bulk of the collections consists of fine specimens of national importance from classic sites throughout Britain.

The acquisition of much of this material was due to just four people – two Keepers, John Phillips and Edward Charlesworth, and two Honorary Curators, William Reed and John Francis Walker. These four formed an unbroken chain of commitment to the Museum, strengthened by personal friendships, from 1826 to 1907. The youngest, John Walker, may well have been influenced as a young man by John Phillips and Vernon Harcourt, both of whom remained actively involved with the Society after they moved to Oxford. With Walker's death in 1907 this link back to the founders of the Museum was broken, and as the Museum moved into the 20th century the geological collections came to be seen as an heritage from the past rather than as an actively evolving department.

By this time the problems of cleaning, conserving and storing the Society's collections had created a vicious circle of neglect, as the amount of work necessary, with limited financial and spatial resources, discouraged those who might have willingly devoted part of their time to a less Herculean task. The Annual Reports show that many of the Honorary Curators chose to immerse themselves in the study of a small area of their

2

subject, rather than tackle the unsatisfactory conditions of the collections in general. The Museum building was developing major defects and was totally inadequate for the storage needs of the specimens, but the Society could afford no more than the cosmetic treatment of new displays, piling the collections meanwhile into basement rooms and balcony shelves.

Only after the Museum had passed into the hands of the local authority was it possible to provide sufficient investment in terms of professional staff and extra accommodation as well as materials necessary to tackle the basic problems of the collections. It would have been impossible for a privately funded Society alone to support expenditure on the Museum which first York Corporation, and latterly North Yorkshire County Council, have found essential.

This book has grown directly out of the author's experience, during the last 20 years, of curating the geology collections of the Museum. Although the Museum has been in existence for over 150 years, until now there has been no comprehensive review of the history of the institution and its collections, and no immediate source of information on those who held posts in the Museum, or donated specimens, or on the conditions of storage and display during the century and a half of the Museum's existence.

During the 19th century the Museum amassed large (over 120,000 specimens) collections of geological material, as well as important biological, archaeological and other collections.

The primary aim of this work is to document the changing fortunes of the geological collections, but neither the Museum nor its parent body the Yorkshire Philosophical Society can be studied in isolation from the effects of local social and economic factors, and we can also see how the Society was both influenced by, and contributed to, the growth of the national scientific establishment.

Previous Research

WITH ONE EXCEPTION VERY LITTLE previous research has taken place into the history of the Yorkshire Museum; and published material consists almost entirely of short articles in the Annual Report of the Yorkshire Philosophical Society for various years.

These include a few brief biographical notes, the subjects being John Phillips (Collinge, 1925; Orange, 1972); W. V. Vernon Harcourt (Owen, 1972); James Atkinson (Barnet, 1972); Thomas Allis (Melmore, 1929) and Charles Wellbeloved (Peacock, 1972); a short review of the founding of the Museum is given by Gee and Willoughby, 1967.

Two longer articles in the Annual Report are of particular interest, as they provide eyewitness accounts of earlier periods. The first (Kenrick, 1873) is of the early years of the Society. The Rev. John Kenrick, a lecturer at Manchester College, then in York, joined the Society at its very beginning and was a Council member by 1827; he remained one of the Society's most active members throughout his long life. His paper, which was read to the Society as it celebrated its first 50 years in 1873, concentrated on the founding of the Society, the acquisition of the land on Manor Shore and the building of the present Museum. He followed the fortunes of the Society up to the 1840's, when the Beckwith legacy of £9,000 rescued the Society from a position of financial embarrassment. The more recent history of the Society, he suggested, was 'fresh in the memory of the great body of our members' and did not need repeating, thus unfortunately denying later generations the benefit of his recollections.

In the 1970's another member, Dr. E. W. Taylor, looked back to the period 1900-1914 (Taylor, 1972). Dr. Taylor was brought into this world by Dr. Tempest Anderson, one of the most famous benefactors and leaders of the Society, and thus was almost a 'birthright member'. He recalled the atmosphere of the Museum with its gas-lit lecture hall and old-fashioned displays, and schoolboy adventures in the ruins of St. Mary's Abbey.

A catalogue of geological Type specimens was published by Platnauer (1891, 1893) and a brief résumé of the geological collections was published

4

by Melmore (1945-6) as an introduction to his catalogue of Type fossils. Omissions and inaccuracies in Melmore's catalogue, plus research into the Museum's collections in the intervening years necessitated the publication of a new catalogue (Pyrah, 1976-9) and a short article in the Geological Curators' Group Newsletter series on Collectors and Collections (Pyrah, 1974) uncovered further information on some of the collections represented (Torrens, 1974, 1975).

Mention must be made of a paper by a previous Keeper of the Museum, the late George Willmot, read at the Museums' Association conference in York in 1953. It is to this and many conversations with its author that I owe much of my interest in the subject. From these discussions it became evident that Willmot's interest in the subject was not necessarily scientific, and the purpose of his address was almost certainly to amuse and annoy, as much as anything else.

The one detailed piece of research covers the founding and first 25 years of the Y.P.S. In *Philosophers and Provincials* (1973) Orange studied the origins of the Society, its founders and the progress of the Society and its Museum until 1844, with a particular emphasis on the role played by the Society in the founding, in York in 1831, of the British Association for the Advancement of Science, and its return visit to York in 1844.

A brief preliminary study of the history of the biological collections of the Museum was published by the Keeper of Biology, Colin Simms, in 1972, and Peter Addyman's valuable article *Archaeology in York 1831-1981* (1981) outlines the Museum's involvement with that subject over the years.

Sources of Information

THE PRIMARY SOURCES OF INFORMATION have been the manuscript records of meetings and correspondence relating to and preserved by the Yorkshire Philosophical Society. A record of Society business is published each year in the Annual Report, together with lists of donations to the Museum. Both the Society and the Museum hold correspondence from various periods.

The Phillips archive in the Oxford University Museum contains over 60 letters relevant to the Y.P.S., these have been transcribed and copies are held in the Yorkshire Museum.

The newspapers of the period also provide detail about meetings of the Society. Other sources, both published and unpublished, are introduced as they occur in the text, and a full bibliography is given at the end.

Acknowledgements

I ACKNOWLEDGE WITH GRATEFUL THANKS the assistance of the following people and institutions, in providing access to materials and information in their care, and in some cases for personal reminiscences.

Mr. T. M. Clegg and Mr. T. Suthers, lately Curators of the Yorkshire Museum, and Mr. B. Hayton, its present Curator, and the North Yorkshire County Council Library, Archives and Museums Committee, for encouragement and assistance.

The Yorkshire Philosophical Society, and their Clerk until 1987 Mrs. H. F. Lobley, for access to their archives.

Dr. M. Smith (now retired) and his staff in the York Reference Room of the York City Library, for access to their comprehensive indexes.

Dr. R. Greene and his staff at the York City Art Gallery, and the Librarian, *Yorkshire Evening Press*, for help in supplying illustrations.

Also the following:– Miss A. L. Arthur, Wisbech and Fenland Museums; Miss B. Balcarres, Oxford University Museum; Dr. H. W. Ball, British Museum (Natural History), London; Dr. J. Bellamy, University of Hull; Miss P. M. Butler, Ipswich Museums; Dr. M. A. Calver, Institute of Geological Sciences, Leeds; Mr. P. S. Clasby, Lymington, Hampshire; Mr. E. W. Cooney, University of York; the late Mr. J. M. Edmonds, Oxford University Museum; Dr. G. F. Elliott, British Museum (Natural History); the late Mrs. J. M. Eyles, Great Rissington, Gloucestershire; Dr. C. I. Forbes, lately of the Sedgwick Museum; Mrs. R. Freedman, York Archives; Dr. T. Getty, Portsmouth Museums; Misses B. and R. Copinger Hill, Saxmundham, Suffolk; Dr. W. J. Kennedy, Oxford University Museum; Mr. R. A. D. Markham, Ipswich Museums; Dr. C. P. Nuttall, British Museum (Natural History); Dr. L. Royle, University of York; Mr. K. J. Spencer, Institute of Geological Sciences, London; Mrs. M. Thallon, York Archives; Dr. H. Torrens, Keele University;

7

Mr. A. M. Tynan, Hancock Museum; Mr. G. G. Watson, Middlesbrough Recreation and Amenities Department; David Whiteley, University of York.

My sincere thanks are due to Mr. G. Lewis of the Department of Museum Studies, Leicester University, and Dr. T. D. Ford, of the Department of Geology, Leicester University, for their patient discussion and helpful criticism.

Publication was made possible by generous financial assistance from the Geologists' Association, Sessions Book Trust, the Yorkshire Philosophical Society and the Sheldon Memorial Trust.

CHAPTER 1

Historical Background (1684-1820)

IT CAN BE ARGUED THAT EVEN without the particular influence of the Kirkdale Cave bones any Philosophical Society which arose in York would have had particular geological interests, because of the period into which it was born.

The science of geology was created in the period of 1775-1815, from the legacy of the 17th century philosophers (Porter, 1977). Studying physics, chemistry and astronomy, not only had they discovered many of the physical laws which govern the universe, but they had also originated the idea that, in the act of creating the world, God had ordained a set of laws by which it should be run, so that his personal intervention was not necessary for every natural event.

This marked a fundamental change in western philosophical thought. It was accepted that no man could understand the mind of the Almighty, but here was a set of laws for the running of our Earth which could be observed, studied and understood by philosophers, although the reason for their existence may be inscrutable. The discovery of these laws would, it was hoped, assist in the interpretation of God's will as revealed to Moses and recorded in the Holy Testament.

However, the philosophers who were studying the Earth were working in isolation, with a background of commonly accepted geological 'facts' which were largely mythical. The societies they founded tended to be short-lived, and they left no disciples to directly carry on their work. In 1684 York's own Martin Lister outlined a plan for a geological map of England, but Robert Hooke in a posthumous publication in 1705 recognised that the attempt to understand the Earth was 'a vain attempt, and not to be thought of till after some ages past in making Collections of Material for so grand a Building . . .'.

9

This could not be accomplished until the necessary facts could be accumulated, and, as importantly, not until the various studies of rocks, fossils, minerals, and of geographical and geological features and processes were seen to be inter-related as the science of geology.

By the end of the 17th century the Newtonian view of a stable solar system governed by physical laws rather than by God's day-to-day will reinforced the idea that the Earth was also basically stable and unchanging, except for divine intervention such as the Noachian flood. In the light of such ideas the evidence seen in the rocks was largely inexplicable, and, following Hooke's suggestion, the philosophers retreated from attempts to create cosmogonic theories, and concentrated on building up the necessary archive of observed facts by which the theories could eventually be tested.

During the first three-quarters of the 18th century the progress of science was practical rather than philosophical, as the physical and chemical discoveries of the previous century were turned into the chemical and engineering principles on which the industrial revolution was built. This period is often seen as one of the decline of scientific investigation, 'a sterile interval between Newton and Dalton' to quote Porter (1977), but Porter demonstrates that it was rather a period of quiet consolidation, not dominated by great scientific personalities, but one which saw:

'the upsurge of indigenous, middle-class, provincial culture; practical, rational, scientific in outlook, and associated with commercial and industrial enterprise.'

This quiet study of detail, rather than grand theorising, presented no threat to the religious cosmogonies, and therefore aroused little interest among the clergy. When, at the end of the 18th century the success of the industrial revolution, with its increasing demand for coal, iron and other raw materials, began to focus attention on the natural resources of the Earth, few of the geologists who took up the challenge were churchmen. The Geological Society of London was founded in 1807, with a diplomatic emphasis on practical and economic, rather than theoretical, geology which enabled it to unite in its membership followers of opposing geological theories (although in the event it generated its own internal controversies; see Weindling, 1979). None of the founder members was in Anglican orders: 'the group was notably non-academic and non-clerical' (Porter, 1977).

This period also saw, for the first time, the formation of specialist provincial societies, founded not in the traditional seats of learning, but in the centres of industrial and mining growth, and drawing their membership not from an elite group of friends, as had the 17th century societies (and the Geological Society) but open to all with a philosophical or practical interest

10

in the subject. The Newcastle Literary and Philosophical Society, founded in 1793, and the Royal Geological Society of Cornwall, founded in 1814, were examples of successful provincial societies founded on the scientific and economic aspects of mining geology.

At the same time, increasing revolutionary activity on the Continent led to a strengthening of conservative clerical views in England, as churchmen and politicians sought to contain social discontent within the framework of humanitarian Christianity. Gillispie, in *Genesis and Geology* (1951) shows how this brought geology and religion into opposition. Mineralogy and geology lectures were introduced at Oxford in the 1780's, and at Cambridge in 1792; until the middle of the 19th century geology was to remain the most popular science subject, although there was no curricular incentive to attend any science lectures. While the theologians were attracted by the possibilities which geology apparently provided for a greater understanding of the processes of creation, they could not tolerate the new geological theories which tended to remove God from the central role as Provider and Arbiter of human life, which they saw as necessary for social stability. On the other hand the geologists, while determined to work primarily from the evidence of the rocks, were well aware of the social and moral dangers of undermining the religious basis of the structure of society (Brooke, 1979).

The resulting debate, combined with other factors such as the romantic revival, which, in contrast to previous fashions, regarded untamed natural scenery with an appreciative artistic eye (Pointon, 1979), and the nature of geological observation, which can be carried out without the necessity for complex instruments or technical expertise, resulted in geology becoming not only 'the dominant and most brilliantly successful science of the first half of the [19th] century' (Lovejoy, 1909, in Gillispie, 1951) but also one of the most popular sciences, to the extent that it was even regarded as a suitable science for ladies.

Up to this point all attempts to understand geology were based on a study of rocks and minerals. The true nature of fossils had only slowly been accepted. Their value as stratigraphical tools was suggested in Britain by William Smith, at the same time as Cuvier was working on his monumental *Recherches sur les ossemens fossiles de quadrupèdes* (Cuvier, 1812) and Lamarck on his *Histoire naturelle des animaux sans vertèbres* (Lamarck, 1815-1822); thus giving the early 19th century geologists the taxonomic base necessary for palaeontological research.

Smith's reputation as a brilliant civil engineer who could succeed where others had failed, lay in his understanding of the effect of geological and soil structures on land drainage, water supply, building foundations and

11

transport systems, and his work provided a practical demonstration of the economic utility of geological research.

Within 25 years geology was to move from Smith's first map to the detailed maps of the Geological Survey which, with only minor revisions, remained the basis of British geological research for the next century. The history of geology during this period is well documented by e.g. Zittell (1901), Mather and Mason (1939), and in particular Gillispie (1951).

Thus the 19th century popular passion for collecting natural history objects, itself partly a result of the greater wealth and leisure of the middle classes due to the industrial revolution, together with safer and faster travel, and printing techniques which made available accurate and attractively coloured natural history books (Allen, 1976) was reinforced, in the case of palaeontology, by the knowledge that the collection of fossils, and the information to be derived from them, would be of assistance to the pioneers of British geological surveying.

The rapid change in the state of geological research was matched by a change in emphasis in the societies which were springing up throughout Britain. At the beginning of the century the trend was for such societies to be 'Literary and Philosophical', devoted mainly to the presentation of papers about members' individual observations and experiments. By the 1820's the collection of natural history objects into a museum was becoming an accepted function of a society; the Yorkshire Philosophical Society emphasised its scientific aspirations by omitting the customary 'Literary' altogether.

Within another 20 years fashion was to move on to see the emphasis fall on the formation of field natural history societies, in which field collection of specimens, their preservation in a museum, and the presentation of scientific papers were all seen as society activities.

As has been shown, the strong geological interests of the early Society can be explained by reference to the scientific and religious environment of the time, as can the high proportion of clergy (25%) among the early members. That the Society continued to develop along geological lines, despite the fact that the area around York itself is geologically unrewarding, is more surprising.

Unlike the museums at Whitby and Scarborough there were no important fossiliferous localities nearby to provide material for the collections. The presence of active geologists within a society was no guarantee of support for its museum; both the Geological Society of London and the Yorkshire Geological Society abandoned their museums after only a few years. York did not have the industrial and mining connections of Newcastle, Leeds and Sheffield, nor the foreign trade of Hull, Manchester and Liverpool.

Although the Society was founded around a geological collection, Orange (1973, 1981) shows that this was but the final incentive to a movement which had been afoot in York for a few years previously; indeed, a 'York Literary and Philosophical Society' had briefly appeared a year earlier.

The main aim of the Society was to be philosophical study; the Museum, like the Library, was seen by all as an essential aspect of the Society's work, but only some members, presumably those with a personal predeliction for collecting and preserving objects, became involved in its day-to-day running.

The continuation of the Museum, and specifically of the geological collections, and the growth of the latter into one of the major British geological collections, seems to have depended on the individual personalities – or eccentricities – of those who were drawn into the service of the Society on a voluntary or professional basis.

CHAPTER 2

The Foundation of the Society and Museum (1821-1823)

Kirkdale Cave

By 1822 there had for some time been a call from the York press for the formation of a literary and philosophical society in York – and the emphasis was on philosophical subjects – to halt or even reverse the downward trend which had affected York since a combination of restrictive trade practices and lack of local mineral resources had driven innovative industrial business from the City to the coal fields and mill towns of the West Riding. The recently founded societies at Leeds, Sheffield, Whitby and Hull were seen by the editor of the *Courant* as a reproof to the tardy scientific spirit of York residents.

There was no lack of possible support, as there were some 50 seats of superior families within 10 miles of York, several of whom had already formed small collections of geological or antiquarian objects, often saved from the workman's spade during the course of land drainage or building work. One such geological collection was made by the Rev. Thomas Egerton and includes a Carboniferous shark tooth, YM480, inscribed 'The gift of Wm. Croft 1791 June 4th' while two elephant molars in the Museum's collections, donated by W. Whytehead in 1825 bear labels 'Zoolithicus Quadripedis Elephantis dens molaris' and 'a fossil grinder of an elephant found at Hornsea A.D. 1780'.

All that was needed was a satisfactory stimulus; one which would not only bring together a group of people with the right mix of enthusiasm, dedication and social (and moneyed) contacts, but which would also provide an infant Society with purposeful contact with the larger scientific community, outside the confines of York City walls.

This was to come with the discovery, in 1821, of Pleistocene bone deposits in Kirkdale Cave, a previously unknown cavern which had been

14

uncovered by quarrymen, and was, indeed, rapidly being destroyed by their activities. The history of the discovery of this cave and its enclosed fossils has been frequently documented, most recently by Boylan (1981a). The interest of the fossil bone material was first realised by John Gibson, of London, who was visiting the Kirbymoorside area in June 1821. During that summer the cave was excavated by several amateur geologists, including William Salmond of York and the Rev. William Eastmead of Kirbymoorside, the Rev. George Young and John Bird, of Whitby. By November the word of the cave's existence had spread to Oxford, whence came the Professor of Geology, William Buckland, to examine the specimens.

Salmond largely excavated and mapped the cave, accompanied by Eastmead, and made the specimens, plans and other information available to Buckland when the latter visited Kirkdale (Eastmead, 1824).

Buckland's daughter claimed that his visit was instigated by the Archbishop of York's son William Vernon Harcourt but this is not borne out by a letter written by Buckland to Vernon Harcourt on 25th February 1822 which starts:

'Dear Sir, Recalling the attention you were so good as to pay when in Oxford to my lectures in Geology, I beg to forward to you an abstract of my paper on the Kirkdale Cave . . .'   (In E. V. Harcourt, Vol. 13)

From this, it would seem unlikely that Buckland had had any contact with Vernon Harcourt since the latter's student days in 1814, and Buckland's own recollection, that he visited the cave on the advice of Shute Barrington, the Bishop of Durham, seems more reliable.

For Buckland, already familiar with continental bone caves, his study of Kirkdale Cave was a challenging experience, as he realised that he was standing in what had been a hyaena den, the floor 'paved with the bones and teeth of hyaenas, many of them polished and worn by the trampling of their successive generations . . .' and that many of the cracked and splintered larger bones represented the meals of the den's inhabitants, rather than a jumbled accumulation of bones of dead animals washed in by the Biblical Deluge. This sparked off a research programme in which he revisited the European bone caves and carried out feeding observations on living hyaenas.

As a result of this he published the revolutionary theory that these remains were not direct relics of the flood, the carcasses of animals from tropical countries washed into European caves by the power of the global deluge, but rather the fossilised skeletons of animals which had lived and died over a long period in the caves in which their remains are now found.

15

The Biblical Deluge was seen as the force which had exterminated them from Europe and had entombed their remains in layers of silt in the caves where they had died (*Reliquiae Diluvianae*, 1823).

Throughout his geological career Buckland always managed never to be too far ahead of his time, and in 1823 the concept of the Noachian flood was yet to be soundly challenged. What he did however was to set the study of Pleistocene geology free from Biblical interpretation, by demonstrating that the 'antediluvian' semi-fossilised bones from Kirkdale and elsewhere were not the remains of animals living at the time of the flood whose bones had been washed into their present position by the force of that terrible catastrophe, as was the general view of the time. Rather, he opened the shutters on a picture of Europe inhabited in 'pre-diluvial' times, by races of animals – hyaenas, elephants, etc., which for many generations lived and died where their remains are now found.

Reliquiae Diluvianae became the centre of controversy between the theologists, who could not stomach Buckland's reinterpretation of one of their most powerful geological sources of evidence for the flood – the bones of its victims – and the more forward-looking geologists, who disagreed with Buckland's continued belief in a catastrophic flood, which he saw as necessary to explain geological phenomena which must have needed an agency more powerful than natural rates of weathering and erosion. Buckland himself was to help provide the answer to this problem less than 20 years later when he collaborated with Agassiz in the study which recognised glacial phenomena in England (Boylan, 1981b).

The bones from Kirkdale Cave were spread widely among institutional and private collectors (Boylan, 1981a). Much of the material went out of the county, some abroad, while collections were donated to the new museums at Whitby and Hull, but a large portion came to York with William Salmond of York, who had mapped the cave and was reputed to have the largest collection.

Kirkdale Cave proved a stimulus both to the formation of philosophical societies in Yorkshire and to the study of bone caves and other Pleistocene remains in general; in the case of the Yorkshire Philosophical Society, it ensured that the Society's museum was to be seen from the very beginning as a repository for carefully collected series of objects preserved for scientific study, rather than as a 'cabinet of curiosities', and it also gave them a patron, in the person of William Buckland, who not only was one of the leading geologists of the day but also had a personal interest in the scientific importance of their collection.

The Founders of the Society

William Salmond (1769-1838)

Colonel William Salmond was a gentleman of private means. There seems to be little evidence as to his geological interest prior to the discovery of Kirkdale Cave. He paid a team of workmen to excavate the cave, and accompanied by the Rev. W. Eastmead, mapped the cave, producing the plan used by Buckland and by Eastmead in his *Historia Rievallensis* (1824) (in which Eastmead explained that the exploration was not carried out under scientific conditions as strict as later researchers might have wished).

Salmond was elected to membership of the Geological Society in 1823, and evidently became known in London geological circles; when he attended one of Lyell's lectures at King's College in 1832 the great geologist, for whom the lectures were to bring public fame, wrote to his sister that 'Dr. Buckland, De la Beche, Col. Salmond' etc., were among the audience (Wilson, 1972).

Salmond was a Vice-President of the Society in 1824 and 1825, and again in 1829 and 1830. Until the end of 1825 he was also Honorary Curator of Geology, jointly with the Rev. J. B. Graham. The specimens donated by him to the Society during its early years tended to consist of suites of rock samples as well as fossils, and in 1829 he helped William Vernon Harcourt and John Phillips excavate the bone deposit at Bielsbeck (Vernon, 1830).

He resigned from the Society in 1830, but he seems to have maintained an interest in the Museum, as in 1835 he wrote from Rokeby, near Barnard Castle, to Phillips about a donation for the Museum (O.U.M. 1835/24.5), and on his death his remaining Kirkdale Cave specimens were purchased by the Society.

Strangely, although he was made an honorary member of the Whitby Philosophical Society, he was never so honoured by the Society which he had helped to found: that might have been expected, had his resignation been merely due to a change of residence.

James Atkinson (1759-1839)

Surgeon to York County Hospital, and author of a somewhat eccentric Medical Bibliography, of which only the first volume was published, James Atkinson's interest in Kirkdale Cave came from his studies of osteology, and his main contribution to the new Museum was his own collection of zoological and comparative anatomy material, which he promised to enlarge as opportunity occurred, to provide 'an illustration of Physiology and Zoology, and a standard of comparison for Fossil Osteology'.

Atkinson played an active part in most aspects of the Society's administration, and particularly in the zoological department, almost until his death.

Anthony Thorpe (1759-1829)

Thorpe was a solicitor with an interest in antiquarian and literary matters. He was one of the founders and President of the York Subscription Library, and had contributed towards Hargrove's *History and Description of the City of York*, published in 1818. Thorpe had no particular involvement with the geological collections, and played only a minor part in the management of the Society, but it was perhaps through him that the Society obtained the services of his partner's son, Jonathan Gray, as Treasurer, a post which was to be passed from father to son through three generations over the next century.

It is interesting to speculate on why it was these three men, rather than others who also had collections of Kirkdale material, who came together to form the Society and the Museum. Between them, the three could muster a fine collection of Kirkdale Cave remains and experience of practical geological research (Salmond), a fine collection of comparative bone material and a wide range of social contacts in and around York (Atkinson), and considerable antiquarian knowledge, plus legal and financial acumen (Thorpe).

Perhaps the Colonel, William Salmond, who later pointed out to Lord Milton that it was he who proposed the plan to the other two, possessed that organisational ability encouraged by military service and chose his partners in this enterprise with particular care.

The fourth member of the Society was to bring not only young blood to this group of older gentlemen, but also contacts in very high places indeed. William Vernon Harcourt claimed that the idea of the Society was suggested to him by Buckland, and it is possible that Buckland may have suggested Vernon Harcourt to Salmond. Buckland must have been in contact with Salmond by November 1821, when he visited Kirkdale, and, as we have seen, had renewed his acquaintance with Vernon Harcourt early in 1822, so was in a good position to see the potential to the new Society of this well-connected young man, whose geological interest as a student had so impressed him.

William Venables Vernon (Harcourt) (1789-1871)

William Vernon (pl. 1) was the fourth son of Edward Vernon, the Archbishop of York (previously Bishop of Carlisle), and grandson of the

18

Pl. 1.   William Venables Vernon Harcourt. Date and artist unknown

19

first Lord Vernon and his third wife, who was the sister of the first Earl Harcourt. He was one of 11 brothers (and with five sisters) and could boast of 78 first cousins. The potential for historical confusion caused by such a large family was added to in 1830 when William, Earl Harcourt, died, and Edward Vernon succeeded to the family estates in Oxfordshire and elsewhere. Edward Vernon changed his name to Edward Harcourt; his elder sons tended to follow his example, William choosing to be known as William Vernon Harcourt. The estates passed from his father first to an elder brother, but when, in 1861, they came to him, William had to drop the Vernon and from then on was known as William Harcourt.

William Vernon Harcourt should not be confused with his nephew, Augustus John Vernon Harcourt (1834-1919), a chemist of some repute, who worked at the chemistry department of the Oxford University Museum on rates of chemical action and coal-gas purification, among other topics, and was elected as a fellow of the Royal Society in 1863; he was President of the chemistry section of the British Association in 1875. Augustus may have been encouraged in his chemical researches by his scientific uncle.

It is perhaps not entirely irrelevant to mention that William Vernon Harcourt was the father of Sir William George Granville Venables Vernon Harcourt, who rose to be a senior statesman of Gladstone's Liberal Party, serving his country at various times as Solicitor-General, Home Secretary, and Chancellor of the Exchequer, in the 1870's to 1890's.

William Vernon was born at Sudbury in Derbyshire, and after early tutoring at home, was enlisted as a midshipman in 1801 at the age of 12, on board the H.M.S. Theseus under Captain Bligh. His father wrote to the Captain that as two of his elder brothers were studying for Holy Orders, he did not wish to allot 'more than a certain share of the preferment in my patronage to my own family' despite William's desire to enter the Church. The financial problems of raising a large family may have played a part in the Bishop's decision to set William to follow the family tradition of naval service.

William's letters home during the five years he was at sea, mainly in the West Indies (E. V. Harcourt, Vol. 13), show not only considerable intellectual ability but also a strong sense of compassion for the plight of the 'native' peoples, still in slavery. He found the life of a sailor extremely uncongenial to his temperament, although he applied himself to the task with determination, and when, in 1806, upon the death of his elder brother Edward, his father wrote to Captain Bligh, the latter had no hesitation in recommending that William should be released from the Service to follow his original desire.

The midshipmen were tutored in the classics while on board ship and William made a collection of recent shells from the West Indies. Despite his concern at the loss of five years' education, William impressed the Dean of Christ Church, Oxford, with his classical knowledge, and was elected a student of the College in December 1807. He graduated with second-class honours in 1811, and gained an M.A. in 1814. As has already been mentioned, he attended Buckland's geological lectures, and also those of Dr. John Kidd on chemistry. Friendships with the chemists William Wollaston and Humphry Davy also date from this period, and his subsequent career was to follow two separate paths, of scientist and churchman; neither was to be neglected at the expense of the other.

In 1807, Vernon's father became Archbishop of York, and moved to the Palace at Bishopthorpe. When Vernon left Oxford in 1814 he was ordained and inducted a Vicar of Bishopthorpe and Chaplain to his father. In 1824 he was appointed Canon Residentiary of York Minster and Rector of Wheldrake.

After several moves in Yorkshire and Southern England he settled in Bolton Percy, near Tadcaster, where he remained until he succeeded to the Harcourt estates in 1861.

Vernon Harcourt became deeply and actively involved in many matters concerning York Minster and in almost all the institutions of a charitable and reformatory character in the area.

As a scientist, his early experiments in the laboratory which he constructed at Bishopthorpe Palace led to a life-long interest in the action of heat upon rocks, and the production of glasses of different compositions and optical characteristics. In the early days of the Yorkshire Philosophical Society, he initiated a series of experiments in which rocks were placed in the iron furnace of Low Moor, Sheffield, for periods of many months and even years; thus anticipating the work on metamorphism which was to cause such a revolution in geology a century later. Roderick Murchison wrote to Vernon Harcourt in October, 1861:

'In truth, I have not read any geological document in my life which has given me such intense (for we both deal in former intensities) satisfaction as your report on the effects of long-continued heat . . .' (Harcourt, Vol. 14)

Vernon Harcourt was elected a member of the Geological Society in 1823, and a fellow of the Royal Society in 1824. He was evidently regarded by his peers as a capable field geologist; in November, 1826, Murchison wrote to him . . .

'. . . I believe it is the contemplation of some distinguished Yorkshire geologists to write a full detail of all the new discoveries in the fossil strata of that coast. I hope you

21

will be that person, and with Mr. Phillips' correct action I am certain that conjointly you can make an excellent paper – it being palpable that Gray and Bird's Survey [i.e. Young and Bird, 1822] is a most inaccurate and unscientific work.'

The incompatibility of his theological beliefs with emerging geological theories may have caused him to turn away from the broader field of geology and concentrate on his geochemical experiments. In December 1831, in a letter mainly about British Association matters, Murchison mentioned his regret that Vernon Harcourt still clung to the belief in Diluvianism, and in 1871, his son E. V. Harcourt wrote to Phillips:

'The only thing of which he was intolerant was any doubt of revealed truth. This always aroused a righteous indignation in him. His last wish almost was to be able to write an answer to the Darwinian School.'

His main contribution to science was undoubtedly his ability to organise, administer and liaise, firstly in the Yorkshire Philosophical Society, and, after 1831, in the British Association for the Advancement of Science. Of his post as Secretary of the latter organisation, he wrote to Phillips in September 1837:

'I will say first that it is the post of all others which, had I been without a profession, I should most have desired to fill, and secondly that, had I felt equal to it with other duties, I would not have given it up.'   (O.U.M. 1837/45.1)

The Foundation and Aims of the Society

The first recorded meeting of the three founders of the Yorkshire Philosophical Society was on 7th December, 1822, at which 'a printed prospectus was read and approved', and Vernon Harcourt was proposed and elected a member. A week later a second prospectus was approved for printing and distribution, this:

'proposed to establish, at York, a Philosophical Society, and to form a Scientific Library, and a Museum . . . chiefly designed to be a Repository of Antiquities . . . and of Geological Specimens . . .'

By 6th January, 1823, a circular was issued, in which the Society, with its Library and Museum, is described as having been formed: this document was issued to the press, and published in full in the local papers. It forms the foundation document of the Society and Museum, being printed in the Annual Report, 1823, with additional paragraphs, under the title, 'Objects of the Society', and from its date is presumably the document on which recruitment of new members to the Society took place throughout 1823. It is reproduced here in full (pl. 2) but the point of particular interest is that the proposed 'Repository of Antiquities . . . and of Geological Specimens' had become a Society whose 'more particular object . . . is, to

YORKSHIRE

Philosophical Society.

In the formation of this Society, its Promoters have had two objects principally in view.

The most general of these has been to establish a Library, by means of which, Persons of various *scientific* pursuits, in different parts of the County, may be enabled to consult expensive Books, on the subjects of their respective studies, which it might not be convenient to them, individually, to purchase; and, for that purpose, a Collection of such Books will by degrees be made, which will consist of the Transactions of Philosophical Societies, Journals of Science, and Works on Arts, Antiquities, and Natural History, especially those parts of it which relate to Mineralogy and Geology: * to be consulted in the Society's Reading-Room, at York, and sent out to Subscribers residing at a distance.

The more particular object of the Society is, to elucidate the Geology of Yorkshire. There are few Counties in England which are traversed by so great a variety of Strata as this, few of which the Strata contain so many Fossils interesting to the Geologist, or so many Minerals important to the Arts, and few of which the Geological relations are so imperfectly and doubtfully determined. Towards the illustration of this subject, the Society presume to hope that something may be done, by the combined observation of many individuals, in their respective neighbourhoods, and by a contribution of Specimens from every part of Yorkshire to a Central Museum.† The foundation of such a Museum has been laid, by a present made to the Society, of a very valuable and perfect Collection of the Fossil Remains lately discovered in the Cave of Kirkdale; to which there have since been added Specimens of the Ichthyosaurus, Plesiosaurus, Ammonites, and other Fossils of the Alum Shale, and of the various Vegetable Impressions, from the districts of the Iron Stone, and Coal.

But though the illustration of Geology is the principal design of the Yorkshire Museum, it will be open also to other objects of Scientific Curiosity,‡ and will be a proper Repository, it is conceived, for those Antiquities, with which the County, and particularly the City of York, is known to abound. Some very curious Antiquarian Remains have been already presented to the Society.

Reproduced courtesy of the Yorkshire Philosophical Society

Pl. 2. The beginning of the 3 page document, dated 6th January 1823, which describes the aims of the new Society and Museum elucidate the Geology of Yorkshire'. 'The illustration of the Geology of Yorkshire' had become 'the principal design of the Yorkshire Museum' and the Library was to collect especially books relating to mineralogy and geology.

A contemporary explanation of this significant shift in emphasis is given by John Kenrick in an address to the Society on its 50th anniversary in 1873. Kenrick (1788-1877) was a brilliant classicist, historian and philosopher of international repute. He held the post of Tutor of Classics in Manchester College, then in York. When the College returned to Manchester in 1840, Kenrick went with it as Professor of History, and later held the post of Principal. His permanent home, however, remained in York. Kenrick joined the Yorkshire Philosophical Society in 1823, and soon became a Council member: he was actively involved both in the research and collections activities, including the geological department, and in the Society's administrative affairs over the next 50 years, and so his recollections, although made half a century later, may be taken as well-informed.

Of the geological emphasis of the newly-formed Society, Kenrick suggested 'In the priority assigned to his favourite science, we may trace, I think, the hand of Mr. Vernon Harcourt.' He then explained the broader aims of the Society:

'Mr. Harcourt possessed advantages for carrying out the scheme of a County Society, which neither of the others enjoyed . . . Various provincial cities and towns – Exeter, Norwich, Bath, Manchester, Newcastle, Leeds, had been the seat of the Societies professing exclusively literary objects or giving only a secondary place to science. The Yorkshire Philosophical Society assumed by its title primarily to represent science, and in making the ancient capital of the north the centre of its operations, paid only a just tribute to its venerable traditions and its position in the yet undivided county.'

The geographical position of York meant that the new society was unlikely to be influenced unduly by one or another of the established centres of learning in the country, and advice and assistance came from various quarters according to the scientific connections of the founders and officers of the Society. The senior geologist of the new museum was William Marshall (Hatfeild), who had been a member of the Geological Society of London since 1817, and presumably introduced Salmond and Vernon Harcourt into that Society when they were elected members in 1823. George Goldie brought Edinburgh connections, and to Vernon Harcourt the Society owed links with Oxford and in particular with Buckland.

While studying at Oxford, Vernon Harcourt had also obtained the friendship of William Conybeare (1787-1857), one of the senior Oxford geologists. After his marriage in 1814 Conybeare left Oxford for Bristol where in 1823, with Sir Henry de la Beche, he helped found the Bristol Institution for the Advancement of Science, Literature and the Arts. Towards the end of 1823 Vernon Harcourt visited Bristol to inspect their museum, and over the next four years specimens and casts of fossils were exchanged between the two societies. Conybeare and Vernon Harcourt were also in correspondence on the subject of the national organisation of science and scientific societies (Morrell and Thackray, 1981).

The Honorary Members of the Society in its founding year included Sir Humphry Davy, John Dalton, Henry de la Beche, Professor J. S. Henslow of Cambridge, and the Rev. George Baird, Principal of the University of Edinburgh, as well as W. H. Fitton, the Secretary of the Geological Society, and William Clift, the Conservator of the Museum of the College of Surgeons, London. By 1824 the list had been expanded to include Adam Sedgwick at Cambridge, several Edinburgh Professors, and the Presidents of the Literary and Philosophical Societies of Leeds, Sheffield and Whitby.

The list of Honorary Members settled down to 50 to 60 British names and a handful of continental 'correspondents', with a strong geological representation, throughout the 19th century. Influence passed from this elite body of membership back to the Society in an indirect manner, via friendships and correspondence with Honorary Curators; thus Thomas Allis, the Curator of Ornithology and Comparative Anatomy, was in correspondence with Buckland, Sedgwick, Audubon, Charles Waterton, R. E. Strickland, William Yarrell and Richard Owen (Orange, 1973). Honorary Members could be expected to donate copies of their publications, and occasionally series of specimens, to the Museum. Thus Buckland donated specimens, books and illustrations, and Professor Daubeny, the Oxford chemist, sent reptile remains from the Stonesfield Slate.

From its beginning the Yorkshire Philosophical Society seems to have had friendly links with the other societies at Leeds (founded 1819), Sheffield (1822) and Hull (1822); indeed, several of the county members, resident in or near these towns, were already members of their local society. These other institutions seem to have had no objection to the new society, formed in the county town, taking for itself the county title (although in the early half of the 20th century Thomas Sheppard, the intensely chauvinist Curator of the Hull Museum, waged a continual battle by correspondence and in the pages of the *Annals and Magazine of Natural History*, of which he was editor, to remove the 'shire' from the Society's title). Joined in 1823 by the Whitby Society, and in 1834 by that at Scarborough the societies of Yorkshire co-operated in exchanging specimens, information on techniques and suggestions for lecture tours.

The Society did look well outside the City of York for support, to those landed gentry for whom historically York always had been the social and business focus. Thus of the 121 subscribing members at the end of 1823, 57 lived in York and 51 elsewhere in the county. The addresses of these 51 are almost entirely on country estates in the Vale of York and on the rich farmlands of the Howardian Hills, with a few from market towns in the area.

This, the natural catchment area of a society based in York, may also be relevant to the geological emphasis of the new society. While the York membership of the Society was drawn from the intellectuals, medical and church men, whose interests in science were shaped by the fashions of the period, the landed gentry in a rich farming area such as the Vale of York had a more practical interest in the study of geology as an agent for the improvement of their land. The fame of William Smith 'the Father of English Geology' had spread north from his native Oxfordshire, and in 1817 he received his first Yorkshire commission, to survey for a canal between Knottingley and Doncaster. From 1820 onwards much of Smith's time was spent in the county, and his four-part geological map of Yorkshire was published in 1821. Furthermore, while the fossils of the coast and the Pennines were available to the casual collector, it was only during the course of agricultural or civil engineering operations that the Pleistocene fossils of the Vale of York were likely to be recovered, and many of the early donations to the Society consist of teeth, horn-cores and bones found while digging wells and drainage canals, or, as in the case of the Bielsbeck deposit, extracting marl for use as manure.

Of 110 papers communicated to the monthly meetings of the Society from 1823 to 1830, 79 were geological in content, 14 dealt with antiquarian topics, and the remainder (17) with various biological or physical observations and experiments. Of these 79 geological papers, 24 were communicated to the Society by members of scientific fame, such as Buckland. Only 10 were contributed by York residents, while 45 came from residents of the county, and were concerned with a wide range of geological topics relating to the geology of the county. No doubt encouraged by Vernon Harcourt, the members were actively pursuing the aims of the Society, which hoped:

'that something may be done (towards the illustration of the Geology of the County) by the combined observation of many individuals, in their respective neighbourhoods, and by a contribution of specimens from every part of Yorkshire to a central museum.'

This input of geological observations, augmented no doubt by many scraps of information not formally recorded must have been of great assistance to John Phillips in the preparation of his two volumes of *Illustrations of the Geology of Yorkshire* (1829 and 1835) and 10 years later Vernon Harcourt was to visualise a similar compilation of observations from individuals, co-ordinated by a central body, as the foundation of the British Association for the Advancement of Science.

This particular emphasis on geological science, which was due to a short-lived combination of scientific fashions, and the particular interest of the founders, catalysed by a major geological discovery in the area (Kirkdale Cave), served in the long term merely to balance the geological department against other departments such as natural history and archaeology which were based on a much surer local footing. In the case of archaeology this was, and still is, provided by the wealth of archaeological material of international importance to be found within the City of York itself, as well as in the surrounding areas, while natural history is well served by a wide range of rich ecological habitats, many within walking distance of the City. These subjects were literally at the Society's doorstep; to find a similar situation in geological terms one would have to look at Whitby or Scarborough, both of which developed geological museums as a matter of course.

Nevertheless, almost all of the salaried Keepers during the first century of the Museum's existence were geologists, as were the majority of Honorary Members. Had geology not been singled out for especial attention in the beginning this continued professional presence would have been unlikely.

Accommodation

The first home of the Society and its Museum was a suite of five rooms in Low Ousegate, on the waterfront next to Ouse Bridge, which was purchased by a group of members and rented to the Society, although by 1825 steps were being taken towards procuring a site on which to build.

Personnel

By 1824 the permanent framework for the management of the Society had been erected. Officers included a President, Vice-Presidents, a Treasurer and one or more Secretaries, and a Council of 12 members. Council had the power to appoint from the membership the Honorary

Curators for the various collections. The Council and Vice-Presidents naturally consisted of a mixture of those deeply involved in the running of the Society and members chosen for their social position, of status value to the Society.

The founders of the Society were involved to varying degrees. Anthony Thorpe became the Honorary Curator of the Library, and the surgeon, James Atkinson, Honorary Curator of Comparative Anatomy. William Salmond took the post of one of the two Honorary Curators of Geology, while Vernon Harcourt was elected President of the Society.

Salmond's colleague in the geology department was the Rev. John Baines Graham, Vicar of the Holy Trinity Church in Micklegate. There is little record of J. B. Graham's interest in geology; only one geological donation is recorded, that of 'fossils' from several strata of the Yorkshire Coast, in 1826. There were also two Honorary Curators of Mineralogy; J. B. Graham's father the Rev. John Graham, Rector of St. Saviour's and St. Mary's and sometime master of Archbishop Holgate Grammar School, and William Marshall.

William Marshall (Hatfeild) 1799-1844

William Marshall, of Newton Kyme, near Tadcaster, was born into a military family. Apparently through his paternal grandmother he inherited the estate of the Hatfeild family of Laughton-en-le-Morthen, and changed his name to Hatfeild in 1833. His obituary in the *Yorkshire Gazette*, 14th September, 1844, states that 'He was a liberal person of the arts, and devotedly attached to scientific pursuits' but no record of his geological interests prior to the formation of the Yorkshire Philosophical Society appears to have survived, although he was elected a member of the Geological Society in 1817. He should not be confused with William Marshall of Pickering, a pioneer of agricultural practices, who died in 1818.

From 1823 to 1843 Marshall donated to the Museum several collections of fossils from localities in Britain, Europe, Egypt and America; of the foreign material, the Egyptian specimens at least are recorded as being collected by himself. During this period no mineralogical donations are recorded, except that in 1832 the Annual Report records 'while far distant from this Museum, the Curator of MINERALOGY had been not unmindful of his peculiar charge' with donations of a mass of native platinum, weighing over 2 ozs., osmium, iridium, etc., from the Urals and further minerals from the Government of Orenburg, and from Siberia. This trip to Russia resulted also in a paper entitled 'An Account of the Russian method of rendering Platinum malleable' which was first presented to the

28

Society on 7th February 1832, and later published in the *Philosophical Magazine*. Marshall undertook to prepare a report on the mining district of Yorkshire for the 1844 York meeting of the British Association, touring through Northern England and collecting specimens for this purpose, but died before its completion. On his death the 'extensive and valuable' collection was donated to the Museum.

John Graham was evidently more geologically inclined than J. B. Graham and the Annual Report records a series of donations to the department during the 1820's and 1830's. These are mainly of miscellaneous specimens, although in 1833 he donated 'A large series of Crag fossils, including almost every published species, and several nondescript [i.e. undescribed] fossils' from near Woodbridge – presumably a purchased collection.

In 1825, Salmond and J. B. Graham retired from the posts of Honorary Curators of Geology, and this department was taken over by John Graham, leaving William Marshall as sole Curator of Mineralogy.

The Secretary to the Society, with various colleagues, for the first few years, was Dr. George Goldie (1784-1853). Goldie, born and bred in Edinburgh, was Physician to York Dispensary, and later to York County Hospital, and in 1831 was in charge of the cholera hospital. A Catholic, one of his sons became a priest and his daughter entered St. Mary's Convent in York. He left York to practise in Shrewsbury in 1832, evidently due to some personal scandal (Goldie to John Phillips, O.U.M. 1832/38.2) but later returned to York, before moving to Sheffield, where he died.

Goldie became a close friend of John Phillips, and the Oxford University Museum's Phillips archive contains a dozen letters, dated from 1824 to 1844, relating to the Society's activities and other York social events.

Goldie seems to have been an energetic Secretary, and it was he, rather than the Honorary Curators, who entered details for some 5,000 fossils into the first geological catalogue, which covers 1823-5.

Other scientifically active members of the Society included the brothers Thomas and James Backhouse, highly competent naturalists who, in addition to running a large and horticulturally famous nursery in York (now the base for York City's Parks Department) had interests in banking and railways. The Backhouses, together with James Atkinson, laid the foundations of the zoological and botanical collections, while the same service was performed for the archaeological department by the Rev. Charles Wellbeloved (1769-1858), the Principal of Manchester College.

29

Wellbeloved's reputation as a classical scholar was such that the College moved from Manchester to York in 1803 to obtain his services. He was Honorary Curator of Antiquities from 1823 until his death, and was responsible for the excavation and publication of St. Mary's Abbey during the construction of the Museum. His *Eburacum or York under the Romans* Addyman (in Feinstein, 1981) describes as 'still a valuable scholarly summary, epitomising the breadth of learning, systematic method and practical approach of Victorian antiquarianism at its best'.

CHAPTER 3

The First Keeper (1823-1844)

BY THE GENERAL MEETING OF 5th March 1823 Goldie had arranged for
details of scientific communications and donations to be recorded in
separate books. However, this seems to refer to a list of donations, rather
than a separate catalogue of individual items – the catalogue preserved in the
department dated 1st January 1823 appears to date in fact from 1824 (see
below). By July the Museum was declared open to visitors, and it was
announced that the Society had followed:

'the manner of arranging and preserving specimens adopted in the Museums of the
Royal Institution and Geological Society which [Vernon Harcourt] had lately
visited.'

By the end of 1823 the officers were able to report that:

'upwards of TWO THOUSAND specimens of Minerals and Fossils, for the most
part illustrative of the Geology of Yorkshire, have been entered on the Society's
Catalogue as gratuitous donations, exclusive of the TWO HUNDRED AND
FORTY FIVE specimens from the Cave of Kirkdale, which formed the
commencement of this part of the Museum.'

This included Pleistocene material from Oreston Cave, Plymouth; the cast
of a jaw of a Plesiosaur from Dorset; 110 specimens from the Oxfordshire
Oolite donated by Buckland; and specimens of Wiltshire and Somerset
fossils donated by Conybeare and Miller. Both Eastmead and Young gave a
series of Yorkshire geological specimens. While Vernon Harcourt gave
some 500 fossils, and minerals from the continent, his brothers Leveson
Vernon and Captain Frederick Vernon also contributed, the former with
specimens from Northumberland and the latter with minerals from South
America. (During the next few years considerable donations were to be
made by eight members of Vernon Harcourt's family.) The Dean of Ripon
donated minerals from the Spanish Royal Mines; Lord Stourton gave
Alpine and Vesuvian minerals; the Earl of Carlisle gave fossils from the

31

Malton Oolite of his Castle Howard estate, and Archdeacon Wrangham donated fossils from the Chalk of the Wolds. Much of the remaining material had been donated by individual members who were to be steady contributors to the geological department of the Society over the next few years.

Correspondence and Council Minutes show that Salmond, Vernon Harcourt and Goldie were active in London on the Society's behalf, purchasing books and specimens at auction, and consulting the Curators of the collections at the Royal Institution and the Geological Society for advice on storing and displaying specimens. These letters were published in full by Melmore (1942); they include the following, both from Vernon Harcourt in London:

'Salmond & myself have been purchasing some minerals for the Society at an Auction which has been going on for the last week, the purchases may amount to some £30 . . . I have been looking at the arrangement of the Geological collection at the R. Institution. The shelves are elevated at a much greater angle & the specimens supported by partitions. The shelves are short and made to take out. The glass coincides with the division of the shelves, the cases are of deal painted oak colour. Would this not be considerably cheaper than oak for our own?'

(26th May, 1823)

'I find from those here who are experienced in Geological collections from Faraday at the Royal Institution and from Mr. Webster at the Geological Society that there is very great difficulty in preserving such specimens from dust. Faraday says that a great part of his time is occupied in cleaning the minerals of the Institution notwithstanding they are kept in cases with glass doors & Webster says that glass doors are no protection unless very particular care is taken in their construction; it is necessary to fit them with bevelled planes at all points at which they open and to cover the bevelled planes with cloth, so that they may be closely pressed together when shut, and this on the side where the hinges are as well as in other parts, and Mr. W. adds that unless the dust is excluded the Geological no less than the Mineralogical specimens are soon spoilt. . .' (2nd June, 1823)

Vernon Harcourt also sought Buckland's advice on both practical and philosophical matters, and the latter's influence on the direction taken by the new Society seems to have been considerable. On 29th December 1822, only 22 days after the first recorded meeting of the founders of the Society, Buckland wrote he was 'much gratified to hear you report such good progress of your Institution' and suggested specimens which should be acquired:

'There is a very fine collection at Scarbro' belonging to Mr. Hinderwell, an elderly gentleman, which would at once set you up if he could be induced to bequeath it to you.'

32

Thomas Hinderwell did subsequently donate some fossils to the Society but his collection, after his death in 1825, formed the nucleus of the Scarborough Museum and Literary and Philosophical Society.

The main part of Buckland's letter consists of a bibliography of 'the principal books connected with English Geology none of which I think you should be without' (Melmore, 1942). Vernon Harcourt later reported to the Society that Buckland had supplied him with the name of the tray-maker from whom the Oxford University Museum obtained their requirements, and also quoted information which Buckland had sent him regarding the geological relationships of the Oolite Series of rock in Yorkshire.

The Society was also particularly encouraged and advised by George Young, the Secretary of the Whitby Literary and Philosophical Society. Young, a Presbyterian minister, had for several years been engaged upon a study of the geology of the Yorkshire Coast, together with John Bird, also of Whitby, and William Bean and John Williamson of Scarborough. Young had also been involved in the exploration of Kirkdale Cave. This work led to a series of publications by Young on the Geology of Yorkshire, from 1817 to 1838, of which the best known is Young and Bird's *A Geological Survey of the Yorkshire Coast* (1822). According to Martin Simpson (1884) it was Young's first publication, in 1817, of *A History of Whitby* which 'immediately produced a general revolution in publick opinion respecting the fossil remains of our district, and excited great zeal for further discovery.' This led by 1823 to the formation of the Whitby Literary and Philosophical Society, with Young as one of its Secretaries and Bird the Curator of the Museum.

Young's interpretation of geological facts was strictly Scriptural, and in *A Geological Survey of the Yorkshire Coast* he ascribed the deposits of Kirkdale Cave to the Noachian flood, but his geological aims were sound; in the preface he explained:

'The chief thing to be done, therefore, in the present state of the science, is to enrich it with ample stores derived from actual observation; to collect information concerning the characters, and relative positions, of the substances composing the solid part of the globe; to specify their arrangement, extent and localities; and notice such hints as they may furnish for elucidating the history of our planet.'

A series of letters from Young to the Yorkshire Philosophical Society, dated 1823-1827, show that Young became the Society's coastal representative, sending boxes of specimens from his own collection and duplicate material from the Whitby Museum, as well as material purchased for the Society from the Whitby dealer Brown Marshall. Some of this material was sent as a gift, some was purchased or exchanged with surplus material from the Yorkshire Museum.

The Yorkshire Philosophical Society could also offer assistance to Whitby; on occasion Young borrowed from the Society's Library, and Vernon Harcourt sent a lithographic press for Bird's use. Young probably also benefitted by being able to put more business the way of Brown Marshall and thus being his chief customer; so being able to reserve the best specimens found by the dealer.

This connection must have been invaluable to the Yorkshire Philosophical Society. The fossiliferous Liassic Beds of Whitby are separated topographically from York by the rugged terrain of the North York Moors; not until 1844 could Council report to the Annual Meeting that:

'The railway now in progress to Scarborough, with its branches to Whitby and Bridlington . . . will greatly facilitate the means of communication with the three richest [fossiliferous] spots on the coast.'

William Smith's Lectures to the Society

William Smith and his nephew John Phillips (pl. 3) were by now in Yorkshire. In November 1821 Smith had given 'a lecture or general explanation of his views on the Geology of Yorkshire' to the Leeds Literary and Philosophical Society (Phillips, 1844). Details of the events which led to the request from the Yorkshire Philosophical Society to William Smith to lecture in York, and the lecture courses in 1824 and 1825 given by Smith and Phillips, are given in Edmonds 1975a; only that which is relevant to Phillips' subsequent employment with the Society is given here.

In January 1823 Smith wrote agreeing to lecture to the Society, and continued:

'With the assistance of my nephew, and the use of your books, your fossils may soon be arranged as the original collection in the British Museum is, both in the stratigraphic and systematic order.'

Vernon Harcourt's original letter to Smith does not seem to have survived. In his reply to Smith's letter he makes no mention of any work to be done on the Society's collections. It therefore seems possible that the suggestion that the Society should employ a professional geologist to help with the collections originated with this letter of Smith's; his motives possibly being that Phillips might gain experience and contacts, rather than any financial reward. It was not until after the successful conclusion of Smith's lectures that the Society voted 'Twenty pounds to Mr. Phillips as a remuneration for the duty which he has undertaken, of arranging the Geological department of the Museum'.

*Pl. 3.   John Phillips, first Keeper of the Museum. A lithograph by
T. H. Maguire, 1851*

In the first catalogue of the geological collection, headed General Inventory and Geological Catalogue, and dated 1st January 1823, the first thousand or so entries are in Phillips' hand – he initialled his identification of the very first specimens – and the book was closed by Goldie in January 1825. It must therefore date from this first period of Phillips' temporary employment early in 1824. Various specimens, including 142 Whitby specimens bought off the dealer Brown Marshall, are listed before Salmond's Kirkdale Cave material is reached at No. 572; this suggests that Phillips may have been listing material as he came to it on the shelves, rather than following an earlier accessions book. While at York Phillips impressed both Vernon Harcourt and George Goldie, striking up a close friendship with the latter, and also renewed his friendship with E. S. George (1801-1830) the energetic chemist and geologist who in his short life was to contribute considerably to the Leeds Society. Phillips and Smith also visited Kirkdale Cave with Salmond.

Both Smith and Phillips were elected Honorary Members of the Society, and after leaving York for the summer sent specimens and geological observations to Vernon Harcourt, and borrowed specimens from the Society for their September lecture course in Scarborough.

Geological material continued to pour in to the Museum, and by November 1824 Vernon Harcourt could report to the members that:

'Professor Buckland had lately visited the Society's Museum, & had appeared much gratified by the illustration which its geological department afforded of the stratification of Yorkshire. The utility & importance to Science, of such local collections had been practically shewn on this occasion; as Mr. Buckland by his examination of the Society's cabinets had been enabled in a few hours to clear up in his own mind several points of great Geological importance; in particular, that the Malton Oolite is identical with the "Coral Rag" of Oxfordshire.'

The Honorary Curator of Geology, the Rev. J. B. Graham, appears to have been unable to cope with the demands of the collection, and Vernon Harcourt was absent for much of the year; by December Goldie wrote to Phillips:

'The section of the Yorkshire Coast which you are so kind as to promise, would be doubly welcome if you would be *yourself the bearer*. Probably this dreary and stormy season will cause some suspension or slackening of your out-of-doors labours, and if Mr. Smith could afford to lose your assistance for two or three weeks, it would give me particular pleasure if you would accept of a bed & give me the favour of your company at my house during that or a longer period. I am doubly interested in making this request, for beside the pleasure of your company in Blake Street, I should give you abundant occupation for your mornings in Bridge Street, in setting to right the numerous *faults & dislocations* which my *vice*-curatorship has produced there, & which I fear would exercise your patience almost as much as those in the Leeds coal-field did that of Mr. George – In the Series of the Scarbro' strata (& indeed in all the Yorkshire ones from the Calc. Grit to the Lias) there is I fear a great confusion in our shelves, or rather a complete *unconformableness*, which asks your helping hand . . .'   (O.U.M. 1824/4)

The next week Vernon Harcourt also wrote to Phillips at Hull, where after giving a lecture course with Smith, Phillips was arranging the Hull Museum geological collections. Vernon Harcourt's letter was to ask Phillips to lecture at York; 'it would give you reputation and put £20 in your pocket . . .' (O.U.M. 1825/1) and Phillips accordingly came to York in February 1825.

By now Phillips' abilities were being noticed outside the county, and in May 1825 Vernon Harcourt, on a visit to the Geological Society in London, was asked by Buckland about Phillips' 'suitability for a post in the Geological Survey of the East Indies' (Vernon Harcourt to his wife; in E. V. Harcourt, Vol. 13).

Phillips spent a certain amount of time at the Museum during the summer of 1825, and impressed Adolphe Brongniart when the palaeobotanist visited the Museum in the autumn (Brongniart to Goldie; in Melmore, 1943b).

John Phillips' Appointment as Keeper

The decision to appoint Phillips Keeper of the Museum was taken by Council on 11th October 1825. By whom this suggestion was proposed is not recorded, nor is there any record of prior discussion as to the necessity for a Keeper. It seems probable that Phillips and the Society had already created a situation of mutual interdependence, which was merely formalised by the appointment. Phillips had already started surveying in detail the geology of the Yorkshire Coast; work which was in complete sympathy with the stated aims of the Society, and the Museum could provide him with a base from which to work, with collections and a library, and the social contacts available in a county town. The Society had come to depend on Phillips' curatorial expertise, and, already planning for a new Museum on Manor Shore, could not risk losing the person who had provided, for the previous two years, a considerable amount of curatorial input, even though on a free-lance basis. Had they delayed much longer they may indeed have lost him to the Leeds Museum; George wrote:

'[Mr. Atkinson] regrets much that we have lost you but I think you could not do better than accept [the Y.P.S.] offer for the present.'   (O.U.M. 1825/4)

The terms of Phillips' appointment indicate the nature of his relationship with his new employers. He was to be paid £60 a year; 11

members of the Society, including Marshall, Vernon Harcourt and Goldie, undertook to subscribe to this salary. In addition he was to continue to gain an income from lecturing to the Society and elsewhere, as he wished. He was expected to attend the Museum on only three days a week, from ten to four o'clock, and was allowed three months leave each year. Thus his duties would not interfere with his lecture tours or field work. In fact during the next few years Council were to allow him further leave for his researches; these included a geological tour of Scotland in 1826, and one of France and Switzerland in 1830.

The new philosophical societies and mechanics' institutes, on one hand, and the popular lecture tours, on the other, were interdependent aspects of the early 19th century popularisation of science. The societies provided the local organisation of the meeting place and list of subscribers for the itinerant lecturer, who would be paid out of the subscriptions of the lecture audience. The difficulties of travel meant that the lecturer would lodge in the town for several weeks while giving his lecture course; he therefore had plenty of time to renew old and make new acquaintances, assist in the local society's museum and examine their latest acquisitions, and pass on information from societies recently visited. The Yorkshire Philosophical Society had already benefitted greatly from Phillips' contacts in this way, and it was to their advantage to encourage him further. As his fame spread his lecture tours were to expand to include Manchester, Birmingham and London.

(The advent of rail links between the major towns in the 1840's put an end to these leisurely extended lecture tours, as it became possible to travel to and from a lecture with only an overnight stop, so that, paradoxically, improved rail travel weakened this strong link between the societies.)

Perhaps most importantly for Phillips, his appointment to York provided a degree of security which for long had been lacking in his life. Orphaned at the age of eight, and taken into the care of his uncle William Smith, he had then, in his own words, 'at too early an age, began to enter the shadow of those calamities in which his revered relative was plunged'. In 1815, the year Phillips left school, Smith faced financial ruin, and had to sell his house and land and even his geological collection. From that point on Smith took lodgings as and where his work took him, and was joined a year later by Phillips as his assistant.

In a long, sad letter, written in 1827 from York to his parents' friends the Armitridings of Steeple Aston, Phillips recalled 'a long vista of sorrowful years' and the 'sorrow & privation & melancholy wandering over the North of England' saddened by the fact that he had not seen his sister Mary for 12 years. In York he felt that he has at last 'the hope of enjoying through God's blessing a contented and peaceful existence' (O.U.M. 1827/6, draft copy).

Phillips took up his position at the Museum early in February 1826, and immediately started a day-book, entitled 'Memoranda of Occupations in which the Keeper of the Museum is engaged'. Although this started with daily entries, it was not maintained; from October 1827 only occasional brief entries appear, and the book was abandoned in November 1828. However, some of the earliest entries give an insight into the state of the Museum's collections after only three years, and the enthusiasm of the young Keeper.

'Feb 9th. Examining the geological collections with a view to its more exact arrangement. Find some of my labelled [sic] antiquated, others soiled, many specimens undescribed, a confusion of arrangement in some cases – revision necessary for all . . .'

'Feb 21st. Rearranged the whole case of Mountain Limestone Fossils – in groups according to geographical position on the principle so long ago recognised when first my hand was put to the Society's conservatorial plough (Feb. 1824).'

'March 11. Cleared some of the duplicate shelves from the literary loads (I mean printed paper) under which they have long laboured – and replaced all the scattered specimens (Mr. Young's series &c.). It is very desirable to exchange *all* the duplicates which are worth sending away, then to arrange the remainder in lots according to the Donors, to whom they may be offered: if refused let them be thrown away.'

'May 16. I think we should have besides our Geological arrangement and Duplicate collection Drawers for a separate systematical arrangement and a separate place for series of specimens which are now lamentably dispersed. A case for rock specimens only.'

'May 30. Concluded the revision of the Mineral Cases and when the corrected catalogue which Mr. Marshall has compiled is transcribed it may be hoped that the Mineral collection will appear respectable and instructive.'

In addition to the geological collections Phillips was also arranging the collections of recent shells and other zoological material, and noted on June 3rd 'Mr. Vernon having allowed a Sturgeon caught at Cawood to be opened for the examination of members I held the dissecting knife'.

By February 1828 Council were able to note that 'The Keeper of the Museum produced a *specimen* of a Methodical Catalogue, which is in progress, of the whole collection of Natural History'.

Phillips was also developing his talents in other directions, both scientific and practical. He demonstrated to the Society, in March 1826, his new design for a 'Lithographic Press with roller and scraper combined in one small cheap frame' and as he became interested in meteorology and astronomy he designed and made much of his equipment. An entry from the diary of John Ford, Headmaster of Bootham School, dated 16th May 1833, suggests that at times Phillips' friends found his enthusiasm difficult to match:

'I breakfasted this morning with my friend John Phillips. I admired his varied and successful application of talent. He makes his own barometers, and with such accuracy of construction that he says he can measure the height of a wall by them. His thermometers are also his own manufacture and he has invented a new form of self-registering thermometer. He has a dipping-needle and one on which he observed the variation of the compass – this morning he says it is 25° west. He has a rain-gauge of his own contrivance which I intend to adopt. In his garden he has a stone tablet with a meridian line drawn upon it. He has telescopes – geological maps of his own delineating and colouring – he is a lithographer and has a turning lathe. I have enumerated the pursuits of my friend to stimulate myself to more diligence in science.' (In Thompson, 1877)

In 1829 Phillips published *Illustrations of the Geology of Yorkshire; or, a description of the strata and organic remains of the Yorkshire Coast*. This was based on many years field-work, first with William Smith and then with Vernon Harcourt, Marshall and others, plus observations communicated by geologists in the Yorkshire Philosophical Society and his friends in the Societies of Leeds, Sheffield, Hull and Whitby. The list of some 400 subscribers was drawn mainly from residents of these five towns, to whom Phillips' lucid style and abilities as an artist and lithographer were already familiar. In addition, no doubt through Vernon Harcourt's connections, the list was headed by the Archbishop of York, four Earls and three Lords.

In his preface Phillips explained the difference between his work and that of Young and Bird, published only seven years earlier, pointing out that he had considered the local strata 'in reference to the general system of geology', and that Young and Bird had 'rejected the principle of identification by the organised fossils, a principle which I consider as the most important yet established in geological science'. Phillips' work also differed from the Rev. Young's text, although Phillips made no mention of this fact, in that he confined his subject strictly to the scientific aspects of geology; there was no place for theological discussion in his work or his publications. It is possible that this precluded any closer collaboration with Vernon Harcourt in publication.

Illustrations of the Geology of Yorkshire was the first descriptive work on the geology of the area based purely on scientific observation without recourse to Scriptural texts; its scholarship was such that, with its companion volume covering the Mountain Limestone district of the

Pennines, published in 1836, it became the standard work on the geology of Yorkshire for almost a century, until Kendall and Wroot's publication in 1924.

Meanwhile the Society was busy excavating on the site of St. Mary's Abbey, next to the King's Manor, on Manor Shore on the Ouse (pl. 4). The acquisition of the semi-derelict area, identified by 1825 as a suitable site for their new Museum, proved to be a complicated process, in which Vernon Harcourt's relatives in the Tory government were able to use their influence on the Society's behalf. A Bill of Parliament was required in order that the land could be made available by grant from the Crown, in 1829. After discussion of the relative merits of the Gothic or Classical styles of architecture, the latter was chosen for the building, designed by William Wilkins.

Careful excavation in the ruins revealed a wealth of archaeological information; the carved stones were eventually displayed in the new Museum while Charles Wellbeloved acted promptly to get the report published by the Society of Antiquaries. From this point on the preservation of the ruins and the gathering of further archaeological material from sites in and around York became one of the Society's central functions.

The conditions of the Crown grant included the proviso that part of the land should be used for a Botanic Garden; part of the land was tenanted. During the next 10 years or so, as the Society gained possession of more land between that originally granted and the River Ouse, further tenanted houses came into their possession, many in a poor state of repair and sanitation. The Society thus found itself in the position of landlord to these poor cottages, a derelict 'Barn' (the mediaeval Hospitium), a swimming pool and, as the gardens were developed, a desirable ornamental area, much in demand for flower shows and similar entertainments. From this time the Council minutes were as likely to be concerned with the state of one of the tenant's drains, or the hire of the marquee, as with scientific lectures or collections.

The cottages were all eventually demolished, and the garden extended from its original three acres to the present area of some ten acres. The Hospitium was repaired, and later restored, and the ruins of the Abbey Church accepted as the responsibility of the archaeology department of the Museum. The swimming pool survived until the early 1970's, although latterly in a derelict condition.

The new Museum (pl. 5) was officially opened in February 1830, having been insured with the Yorkshire Fire Office for £1,500 in a half year. The

Pl. 4. *South East view of the remains of St. Mary's Abbey. A lithograph by F. Nash, 1829. Most of the ruined walls exposed in the foreground were covered by the new Museum, and can be seen in the basement galleries. The Hospitium is visible to the left, while the standing wall of the Abbey Church, to the right of the picture, now forms a boundary wall and focal point of the Museum Gardens and the backdrop to the York Mystery Plays*

42

Pl. 5.   A very early illustration of the Museum. Part of King's Manor can be seen behind the Museum to the left; to the right is the City Wall and the Roman Multangular Tower.   Artist unknown

façade of the building still presents its original appearance, although further galleries were added to the back in 1857 and a new lecture hall was added in 1912. The original lecture hall was in the Central Hall, with tiered seating, surrounded by galleries all with top-lighting by means of clerestory windows. Gas-lighting was installed, and with liberal help from the Honorary Curators, the galleries were fitted out with cases for the specimens.

With his growing reputation as a geologist and lecturer crowned by the successful appearance of his book, Phillips began to look to the further advancement of his career, and by the beginning of 1831 he was being urged by his friends to try for a Chair of Geology at the new University in London. The following letter from George Goldie, in London, to Phillips, dated 31st January 1831, indicates the difficulties which faced a scientist wishing to launch himself on a professional career in London without a private income:

'I have today had a long and important coversation regarding you, with Mr. Leonard Horner [warden at the University of London] . . . the moment I mentioned your name, he was most attentive – & when I stated the possibility of your coming to town on adequate encouragement, his attention became rivetted, and he expressed the most anxious wish that it might be realised – for the sake of Science – of the University – of the Geol. Soc. – of your scientific friends in town – of yourself etc., of whose merits he seems to have imbibed a deep impression from the statements of Sedgwick, Murchison &c but especially from his own conversation with you, & then perusal of your book which he called "a most excellent one" . . . Your election to the Geol. Chair in the L.E.U. he deems a matter of certainty – you can have no rival – for "after Buckland, Sedgwick, Murchison, Fitton &c" he said "who is there" & they are all either precluded or too affluent to seek the office – the reverse of the medal is, the U. now guarantees no salary: that you must entirely depend on the popularity of your lectures . . . What Horner seemed to think most advisable for you to do, (supposing you prepared about April to give a course of 20 or 24 lectures) would be that you shd. make a proposal (it must come from you) to the Council of the L.U. through him, to deliver at your own risk such a course – asking only for their sanction and a lecture-room . . . The result of this course w. (he thinks) be to a *certainty* your election to the Geol. Chair, if on this trial you liked the situation . . . I confess I am strongly in favour of yr. giving the Course of Lectures – however undetermined you may feel as to yr. ultimate removal to London: it can do no harm to make yr. talent more widely known & even we Yorkists will look at you with more reverence as a metropolitan *star* . . . you know as well as I do that you are *utterly thrown away* at York . . .'   (O.U.M. 1831/4)

Phillips immediately agreed to this course of action, and Goldie wrote again a week later with further details:

'He [Horner] thinks you have adopted *quite* the right course . . . You will come here and lecture in April & May – will feel yr. way & extend yr. acquaintances – It will be

44

quite time enough for you to make up yr. mind about the Professorship against Autumn: the Council meet in Novr. when they will elect you, & you will not have occasion to begin the duties of your Chair until Feby. or March 1832. Murchison & Sedgwick are both (teste Horner) delighted at the prospect of having you in London . . .'   (O.U.M. 1831/2)

Goldie went on to say that De la Beche had accepted the vacant post of Secretary of the Geological Society, an honorary position, for the season only with the intention of vacating it for Phillips once the latter had settled in London.

Edmonds (1975b) shows how, despite the subsequent success of his lecture course, Phillips decided to refuse the Chair at Gower Street. London University was being damaged by internal conflict, and Phillips was disenchanted both with the quality of life in London and the jealousy he perceived among the scientists. In addition, on the evening that Phillips gave a lecture to the Geological Society, on his arrival in London, it was announced that a Chair of Geology had been created for Lyell at the rival King's College.

Phillips' decision must have pleased Vernon Harcourt, as Goldie had written to Phillips, as the latter was about to start lecturing in London:

'I had a long argument the other day with Mr. Harcourt in the Mus. Gardens about the motives which might induce you to prefer London as a residence with respect to scientific improvement & distinction. He recurred to all his former sophisms (as they appear to me) in favour of a provincial resident – *perhaps* he believed them: but it was evident that the feeling nearest his heart was the wish to retain you at York . . .'   (O.U.M. 1831/5)

By the end of 1831 Lyell had decided that the Chair at King's College would bring him less fame and fortune than writing (Wilson, 1972); Murchison then wrote to Phillips offering him the post at King's College upon Lyell's resignation, which Phillips accepted, although Lyell did not actually resign until October 1833.

Philips was appointed to the Chair in 1834, and held the post until 1841; the duties were not difficult, consisting of giving one course of lectures during the year.

British Association for the Advancement of Science

In 1830 David Brewster, one of the leading scientists of the time, had written an article in the Quarterly Review in which he attacked the decline of science in England and suggested the formation of an association of 'nobility, clergy, gentry and philosophers' to seek royal patronage for the encouragement of science in Britain.

45

When in February he wrote to John Phillips asking if the new Museum at York could accommodate the proposed meeting, Vernon Harcourt rose to the challenge, and after much hard work by both men, the first meeting of the B.A.A.S. took place in the Yorkshire Museum at the end of September 1831. Lord Milton, who by then was the President of the Y.P.S., became the B.A.A.S.' first President, Vernon Harcourt its Vice-President, and John Phillips its Assistant General Secretary (Orange; in Feinstein, 1981, Morrell and Thackray, 1981).

The B.A.A.S. essentially rose from the same foundations as did the Y.P.S., although its implementation took longer. Morrell and Thackray quote from a letter from Babbage to Whewell, dated 15th May 1820:

'All sorts of plans, speculations and schemes are afloat and all sorts of people, proper and improper, are penetrated with the desire of wielding the sceptre of Science.'

In 1824, when the Y.P.S. was barely a year old, Vernon Harcourt was corresponding with Conybeare on the possibility of co-ordinated researches and lecture tours. As Morrell and Thackray trace the threads which over a decade were woven into the fabric of the Association, Vernon Harcourt's name recurs. They show that in many ways the Yorkshire Philosophical Society was a prototype or trial run for the Association, and was acknowledged as such by Council in the Annual Report of 1831. Vernon Harcourt was doubly lucky in that the Society, in addition to providing a sound launching board for the Association, had also attracted to his side the talented and hard-working Phillips.

The Society had moved into the new Museum at the end of 1829. It was in debt to more than £1,300 on the building fund, and the preparations necessary to house the collections and fit up the rooms sufficiently for the British Association meeting further increased this debt, while their ability to raise money by subscription had been adversely affected by two other public appeals, for the fire-ravaged Minster and for the Hospital. £115 was spent on cases for the geological gallery, but only £20 could be spared for fitting up the laboratory, although the latter situation was remedied in 1833 by a magnificent gift of scientific equipment from the Earl of Tyrconnel.

The provision of cases for specimens proceeded as funds became available, usually as a result of the generosity of individuals, as when in 1834 Phillips gave half the proceeds from a lecture course towards casing for the zoological specimens. However, the collections continued to outgrow the available storage.

Despite this shortfall in the Society's ability to cope with the financial demands of its collections, it expanded into new fields with the erection in 1832-33 of an astronomical observatory in the Gardens, the result of a

46

resolution passed at the York British Association meeting. The subscription for this project also failed to reach the necessary sum, further increasing the debt of the Society. The situation was less than ideal for an observatory, being so near the centre of town, and in an area heavily polluted by industrial smoke from the West Riding, and although it was used by Phillips and others, it failed to gain the interest of the majority of members of the Society. (Because of its historical links and interesting architectural features it has recently been restored and opened to the public after a considerable period of dereliction – see Buttery, 1982.)

The responsibility for the dilapidated Abbey Gatehouse was taken over by Phillips, who leased it from the Society in 1839. He rebuilt it as St. Mary's Lodge, and lived there, on and off, with his sister, until 1853.

The setting up of the Botanical Gardens, aided by gifts of plants from the Backhouses' nursery, and a short-lived menagerie which included monkeys and a bear, also diverted the Society's resources from the Museum.

The bear soon proved too much of a responsibility, and was offered to the London Zoo, whose Secretary, N. A. Vigors, responded with suggestions as to the means of transporting the bear from York to London:

'Zool. Soc. London Dec. 26th 1831.

Sirs,

'We shall feel much pleased in taking your bear on the terms proposed in your letter of the 21st.

'The best mode I can conceive of forwarding him to us is by one of the York coaches, you booking him as an outside Passenger, and promising the Guard a recompense on his delivering him safe in London. Be so good as to send us a line to inform us of the Coach by which the animal is to travel and the place and probable time of his arrival in town. You will also oblige me by stating to whom we shall pay the price of the animal.

'I hope I shall have the opportunity of showing you our Garden, and your old friend as a happy occupier of them.'   (O.U.M. 1831/23)

Unfortunately the Zoological Society no longer has any records relating to this animal; presumably it was a small and friendly bear!

The Y.P.S. Council felt justified in expanding to explore new avenues of popular philosophical interest to attract new members, as, although by 1833 they could boast of a total of 4,000 visitors annually to the Museum, membership subscriptions formed the main source of income.

By 1834, despite the debts, and some aspects of the collections which still required attention, the Society had settled into the new building, and Council could report:

'the great expenses of the institution are now ended; its ordinary charges can be met out of the ordinary income . . . new Members will surely be attracted to share its increased advantages, and to stimulate its growing prosperity . . .'

The geological collections had been brought to the attention of the scientific world by Phillips' *Geology of Yorkshire*, and by the 1831 British Association meeting Allis, whose own interest was ornithology, reported:

'Our Geologists have done themselves and the County great credit by their labours. They have provided us with one of the very best Geological Rooms in the United Kingdom. I believe there is not another room in the Kingdom where a Student in Geology with an elementary book in his hand could with equal facility become acquainted with the science of Geology . . .'

In late summer of 1835 the Society was honoured by a visit of the Duchess of Kent and her daughter Princess Victoria. Their satisfaction at the state of the Society and its Museum was later marked by the presentation by the Duchess of a copy of Goldfuss' *Petrefacten*, the first volume of which had just been published.

As Phillips developed further interests in London and elsewhere, he received much information and gossip about the Museum and York society from various York correspondents, especially Goldie; several letters are preserved in the Oxford University Museum archive.

On 6th March 1837 Phillips wrote to Council asking to be relieved of his office from the end of the year, due to the pressure of work caused by:

'The constant attention required of me as Secretary to the British Association – the Journeys which I am required to make to the places of their meetings, – to perform the functions of my appointment at King's College – and for lectures and other objects connected with my Profession . . .'

(Letter bound in Council Minute Book, 6th March 1837)

After further discussion with Phillips, Council resolved in May that:

'the present state of the Museum does not require the personal attendance of the Keeper as stipulated in 1825.'

and decided that:

'Mr. Phillips be requested to continue his services . . . without any other stipulation than that he shall devote such portion of his time to the Institution as shall be necessary to maintain its collections in proper order.'

This was unlikely to prove a satisfactory arrangement. By May 1838 Henry Robinson was writing to Phillips:

'Mr. William Harcourt is expected down any day and in consequence Baines is getting all things into their order to shew him on his arrival that they are not neglected in his absence . . .'

In 1839 Phillips added to his duties a surveying post with the Geological Survey, and in January 1841 he resigned all his duties at the Museum; later that year he also resigned from the King's College Chair.

Council appointed a sub-committee to report on 'the best manner of providing for the scientific care of the Collections . . .' The report of this committee, which met on 11th January, consisted largely of the report of Phillips to the meeting. He pointed out that there were two alternatives; either to appoint a scientific Keeper to care for the collections, or to nominate Honorary Curators from among the membership. The report continued:

'In adopting either of these plans, Mr. Phillips expressed his opinion that it should be fully *adopted*; that the two should *not be mixed*; if a general salaried Curator be named for the whole or certain parts of the Museum, his direction and responsibility should be unfettered by other nominal or complimentary (called Honorary) appointments; if the several departments be assigned to Special Curators (not merely nominal, but active) these should be severally independent, responsible only to the Council, and allowed free communication with it by written reports or personal application.'

Phillips' verdict on the system under which he had worked for the Society is evident. He went on to suggest that the latter course, of nominating Honorary Curators, would be advisable; among other reasons was:

'the state of the Society's finances, which have not for years been found sufficient to allow of any purchase for the Museum, unless aided by large subscriptions, of which there is reason to believe the Members are now weary. This difficulty has been so great, that the Council has been compelled, most unwillingly, to forgo all attempts to obtain by purchase even one of the many noble fossil saurians which have been discovered on the Yorkshire Coast, or add even a dozen Shells, Corals, or Crustacea, to its imperfect Collections of Invertebrata.'

The sub-committee agreed with Phillips' suggestions, and recommended that each Honorary Curator should be furnished with a list of duties required of him. It was felt that most of the departments were in such a condition that the duties required would not be arduous, except that it might be necessary to employ, for a fixed period, the services of an ornithologist and a 'Erpetologist' 'to place that department of the Museum on a parallel line with the others'.

This document was presented to Council on 18th January 1841. Council agreed to follow its recommendations, but went on to appoint Henry Baines, the Garden Superintendent, in a new position as Sub-Curator of the 'whole Natural History Museum and Library'. He was to attend in the Museum:

'daily from 12 to 4 p.m., and to perform therein such things as shall be directed by the Secretaries and Curators, besides taking care of the safety of the specimens and keeping the order in the Rooms. Before and after these hours, the gardens to be under Mr. Baines' directions . . .'

Baines (1793-1878) had been born, and as a boy had worked as a gardener, in Mr. Suttle's property on Manor Shore. Before being appointed to the position of Gardener with the Society in 1829 he worked for the Backhouses at their famous nursery. He held the position of Sub-Curator until his retirement in 1870, but horticulture remained his first love, and he is remembered for a classic *Flora of Yorkshire* which he published in 1840.

In 1859 he was presented with £200 by the City of York for 30 years service to the community. Under his supervision the Museum Gardens became famous for the hothouses, the giant *Victoria regina* waterlily brought from Chatsworth, and his award-winning insectivorous plants, and formed one of the main attractions of Society membership.

In December 1841 W. Hewetson wrote to the Society asking to be considered for the post of Keeper of the Museum. Goldie wrote to Phillips:

'we apprehend that the appointment which he solicits (& for which I doubt not he is well qualified) would be incompatible with the continuance of Baines' most valuable services on his present footing . . .'

If some way could be found of reconciling these factors Vernon Harcourt would approve:

'as he has always seemed to me desirous of the appointment of "scientific" successor to your former office, and I do not think he altogether appreciates Baines' attainments & usefulness as we do.'

Goldie also suggested that Vernon Harcourt was against bringing the B.A.A.S. back to York in 1843, due to financial problems and 'the paucity of scientific taste and ability in York' although Goldie himself was evidently in favour (O.U.M. 1841/65a.2).

Hewetson's request was taken no further at that time. In 1843 it was decided that the British Association should return to its birth-place the next year, and in November Phillips and several of the officers inspected the Museum 'with a view to make such alterations as would enable them to arrange the collections in a scientific and permanent manner previous to the visit of the British Association'. They decided that various alterations were 'essentially necessary' and that £72 was needed to provide 288 more drawers in the geological room – these were to be fitted under desk display cases in the centre of the room. By February 1844 Council realised that it was 'desirable to appoint a Keeper of the Museum' (Council may have already been aware that they were to benefit handsomely later that year from the estate of the late Dr. Beckwith) and they wrote to Hewetson offering him the post for nine months at a rate of £150 per annum.

Perhaps Hewetson was discouraged by the state of the collections, for on 11th March Council resolved:

'Mr. W. C. Hewetson having declined to accept the curatorship; it is inexpedient at present to appoint a person in that situation until the collections are better arranged.'

Baines was instructed to proceed with this task 'as rapidly as possible' with the assistance of a boy, if necessary, and the appointment of a full-time garden assistant, who would be under Baines' direction.

Poor Charlesworth (1844-1854)

Edward Charlesworth (1813-1893)

Within three weeks of their decision not to appoint a Keeper, Council recorded a:

'Letter accompanied by testimonials having been received from Edw. Charlesworth Esq., soliciting the appointment of Curator to the Museum, and from the said testimonials it appearing that Mr. Charlesworth would be a most eligible person to appoint to the said office . . . a special meeting be called . . .' (1st April, 1844)

The decision to appoint him was taken a fortnight later; the hours were to be four hours a day for five days a week, at a salary of £150 a year.

Charlesworth's contribution to the Museum has never been evaluated, and Orange (1973) dismisses him in the following paragraphs:

'Charlesworth's reign as keeper, which lasted until 1858, is of less immediate interest than the qualifications of the man whom the Council had chosen to appoint. Edward Charlesworth (1813-1893), the son of an East Anglian clergyman and himself educated for the medical profession, had published one significant geological paper (Woodward in his *History of the Geological Society* says that Charlesworth, "a man of great ability and promise", lived on its reputation till the end of his life) and edited the *Magazine of Natural History* from 1837 until the time of his engagement at York.

'If the intellectual ambition of the members of the Yorkshire Philosophical Society was more muted than it had been 20 years before . . .'

In fact the qualifications which Charlesworth could offer to the Y.P.S. were more than equal to those of John Phillips at the time of his appointment to the post 20 years earlier.

Edward Charlesworth was born on 5th September 1813, the eldest son of the Rev. John Charlesworth. While he was still a child his father moved to the Rectory at Flowton, near Ipswich, where Edward was encouraged to collect fossils from the Crag pits in the neighbourhood. He was educated in

Suffolk, and entered medicine, studying at Guy's Hospital, London. However a distaste for medicine led him to return to palaeontology as his overwhelming interest. His sister, Miss M. L. Charlesworth, became famous for her religious publications, which included *Ministering Children* (1854), one of the most widely circulated childrens' books then written, and his uncle, Edward Parker Charlesworth, was visiting physician to the Lincoln Asylum for the Insane, where he greatly improved conditions in the asylum and successfully fought to abolish the systems of restraint and violent treatment then in vogue.

Charlesworth came to the notice of the geological world in style, taking on Charles Lyell in a debate as to the age of the Crag formations. The 38 year old Lyell was by then one of the leading geologists of the day; he had held the Professorship of Geology at King's College, London, before John Phillips, and his *Principles of Geology* was already in its third edition. Lyell thought that the Crag was a single formation; in May 1835 Charlesworth suggested to the Geological Society that there were in fact two, the Coralline and the Red Crag, on the basis of the exposures he had seen at Suffolk, and also of the collection of Mr. Searles Wood (1798-1880) of Hasketon, Suffolk, who also was in favour of there being two beds of Crag. (Charlesworth, 1835a, 1835b.) The heated debate that followed in the pages of the *Philosophical Magazine* and at the 1836 British Association meeting at Bristol is covered in detail by L. G. Wilson (1972, Chapter 14, The Crag Question).

Most of the geologists who had any experience of Tertiary matters were drawn into the discussion, and Lyell went to Copenhagen for several weeks in 1837 to study the matter with Dr. Heinrich Beck, the Curator of Prince Christian's Museum, the best collection of recent shells in Europe. However it was not until 1838 that Lyell went into the field to study the exposures of Suffolk for himself, and what he saw in an exposure at Sutton, laid open especially for him by Mr. Colchester, finally convinced him that Edward Charlesworth was indeed correct in referring the Crag to two separate dates.

Lyell's acknowledgement of Charlesworth's work in his *Elements of Geology* (Lyell, 1838) was not particularly generous, and Wilson quotes the following illuminating letter from Charles Darwin to Lyell, in September 1838:

'Charlesworth, I think, is annoyed that you have not quoted him more . . . but poor Charlesworth is of an unhappy discontented disposition. – He is, moreover, much to be pitied. The Zoological Soc. are going to give up the Ass't. Secretary's place [Charlesworth's position] and it is feared that he has a disease of the heart, so that altogether he is greatly to be pitied.'

Lyell continued to study the problem of the Suffolk and Norfolk Crags, in which he found the various theses postulated by Charlesworth to be correct, and eventually submitted the resulting paper for publication in Charlesworth's own journal, *The Magazine of Natural History*.

During the same period Charlesworth was elected a Fellow of the Geological Society (in 1835); and also became an Honorary Curator of the Ipswich Museum. At that time there were several wealthy private collectors, many of them good amateur geologists, in Suffolk, and undoubtedly Charlesworth counted some of them as his acquaintances.

In 1836 he was appointed to the staff of the British Museum and in 1837 Assistant to the Museum of the Zoological Society of London, when he also took over Loudon's *Magazine of Natural History*. His obituary in the *Geological Magazine* (1893) continues 'in 1840 he left England to take charge of a young gentleman of fortune and travel with him through Central America' while the Geological Society (1894) records that 'The indisposition of his fellow traveller shortened that tour to a few months' duration, and Mr. Charlesworth returned to resume his researches in England'.

A letter from Charlesworth in London to Phillips, in 1841, mentions this trip, and shows that Charlesworth had already had previous contact with the Y.P.S.:

'My dear Sirs,

'I have returned to England after a very pleasant trip to the United States and Mexico, and feel myself vastly benefitted by my 12-month's holiday. My Magazine I parted with to Taylor who has combined it as you are probably aware with the Annals of Nat. History . . .

'Some years ago I supplied the York Museum with a very good series of Corals from the Crag, sent through you with the understanding that I was to receive in return a series of the sponges from the Yorkshire Chalk (Flambro' Head). You promised me several times that the return duplicates should be forwarded to me but I have never received any – If you can obtain these for me without entailing upon yourself trouble or inconvenience I should be glad to have them, but if there be any difficulty about the matter, let the Crag fossils be considered as a donation from me to the Museum – Within the next two months it is very probable that I may be at York, as I propose visiting that part of the Country . . .'   (O.U.M. 1841/27)

In 1842 William Lonsdale retired from the post of Curator and Librarian of the Geological Society, which he had held for 14 years, and Charlesworth applied for the position. H. B. Woodward (1907) in the *History of the Geological Society*, records that the Council decided that he was disqualified from holding office in the Society's establishment.

54

Charlesworth's application was supported by his friends, and a Special Meeting was called, at which there were threats of resignation of some of the leaders of the Society if 'a certain one of the candidates' was elected; Edward Forbes was then invited to apply for the post. Woodward believed that no record of the meeting survived; it is therefore interesting to discover among the Phillips archive at Oxford a letter from the Geological Society Council member Hugh Strickland about this meeting:

'You have probably heard the result of last Friday's meeting. The Council read a long statement, admitting the irregularity of their vote of July 16, but justifying their motives on the ground of Charlesworth's intemperate conduct, both during the original controversy and subsequently, in so much as they quite carried the meeting along with them, and one of C's own requisitionists moved a vote of thanks to the Council.

'Forbes was appointed by the Council, to be confirmed by the Fellows on December 11th and there seems no reason to fear his being rejected by them. So now I hope this unpleasant affair is settled, and I should be most happy to assist Charlesworth to any appointment for which he is fitted, especially if it would keep him quiet, for he is certainly no man's enemy more than his own. Do you think the *Geological Ordnance Survey* might afford him an opening . . .'

(O.U.M. unnumbered 8th December, 1842)

Charlesworth's geological and curatorial abilities were never in doubt – the Geological Society obituary says of this time 'Probably no one rivalled him in arranging and classifying geological collections in museums – work he was often called upon to undertake in addition to his literary labours'. However Woodward (1907) says 'Recognised as a man of great ability and promise, Charlesworth lacked what is usually known as ballast . . .'

Charlesworth took up his position as Keeper of the Yorkshire Museum on 3rd July 1844; the York meeting of the B.A.A.S. was then less than three months away, at the end of September.

It may be safely assumed that Charlesworth and Baines aided by the more active and available of the Honorary Curators, managed to restore the Museum to a reasonable state of order, fit to receive their scientific visitors. Charlesworth indeed went beyond this, identifying and endeavouring to fill the gaps in the Yorkshire Geology series, as the Council Minutes record:

'July 31st 1844. Resolved that £6.3.0 be paid to Mr. Charlesworth for the fossils purchased by him at Whitby, and that he be authorised to proceed to Malton, Whitby, Scarboro and Bridlington to procure such fossils as may be dessiderata to the Yorkshire Series at an expense including his own journey of £30.'

The 1844 York meeting of the British Association was to prove to be a milestone in the continuing battle between scientists and theologians. The early membership of the Yorkshire Philosophical Society included not only those, such as Salmond and Marshall, who were interested in geological discoveries from a scientific point of view, but also those clerics who anticipated that field observations would strengthen the authority of the Bible. The latter included the Dean of York, William Cockburn, and William Vernon Harcourt's older brother Leveson. As the studies of the Society's mentor, William Buckland, and the Keeper of its Museum, John Phillips progressed they moved further away from a strictly Biblical interpretation of geological facts, to the dismay of the clerics.

The anger of the scriptural geologists was particularly focussed on Buckland's contribution to the series of Treatises commissioned by the will of the Reverend Francis Henry Egerton, eighth Earl of Bridgewater, in order to demonstrate 'the Power, Wisdom and Goodness of God, as manifest in the Creation'. Buckland wrote the sixth of the eight volumes in 1836, his subject being geology and mineralogy. Not only had he already shown that fossils were not the result of the Noachian flood, but he also attacked the literal interpretation of Genesis, arguing that its function was to acknowledge God as Creator rather than to give a detailed account of the methods of Creation. Buckland argued that an indefinite time had elapsed between the beginning of the Earth and the six days of Creation, which he believed related only to the creation of Man and the preparation of the Earth to receive mankind.

This drew forth from Cockburn *A Letter to Professor Buckland concerning the Origin of the World* (1838) and from Leveson Vernon Harcourt *The Doctrine of the Deluge, vindicating the Scriptural Account from the doubts which have recently been cast upon it by geological speculations* (1838). Cockburn also published *A Remonstrance, addressed to his grace the Duke of Northumberland upon the dangers of Peripatetic Philosophy* (1838) to warn him of the dangers of presiding at the 1838 British Association meeting at Newcastle, arguing that 'these annual assemblies of Thespian Orators . . . have been, and are likely to be, injurious to religion'.

At the 1839 meeting Vernon Harcourt successfully poured oil onto the troubled waters, but when the Association met in York in 1844, at the invitation of the Yorkshire Philosophical Society, Cockburn, on home ground, delivered a fresh attack, which he published under the title of *The Bible defended against the British Association* (1844). Buckland, who was not present, was ably defended by the Yorkshire geologist Adam Sedgwick, in a speech which lasted for 90 minutes.

This meeting of the Geological Section, which attracted much public attention, was held in the 'old barn', the Hospitium, newly refurbished from a state of dereliction by the Society for the meeting (pl. 6). The

Pl. 6.   *The Hospitium. A mid-19th century view by H. Cave. The Museum and York Minster can be seen in the background*

controversy simmered on for the rest of the week. York Corporation decided they could not entertain both the Dean and the visiting geologists to a dinner, and withdrew their invitation to the latter, George Hudson, the Lord Mayor and 'railway King' informing them 'We've decided for Moses and the Dean'.

The Philosophical Society, although it hosted the event and supplied several of the protagonists, avoided association with the controversy. Although Cockburn and Leveson Vernon Harcourt were less involved in the scientific work of the Society than were Phillips, William Vernon Harcourt and Kenrick, Cockburn was one of the early Vice-Presidents of the Society, and a powerful man in York, despite (or perhaps because of) having been found guilty by the Archbishop of dealing in Church offices. The political dictator George Hudson, who aligned himself with Cockburn, ran both his railway company and the city by corrupt means (Peacock and Joy, 1971; Peacock, in Feinstein, 1981).

If the Y.P.S. had allowed itself to become involved in the controversy it could have had serious consequences for its stability. Vernon Harcourt was at heart a Scriptural geologist, while Phillips was essentially scientific in his approach to the subject. Nevertheless they had worked together closely since the 1820's for the good of both the Association and the Society, and it may have been due to their influence that the Y.P.S., while hosting this explosive meeting managed to keep its distance from the controversy.

Charlesworth's contribution to this meeting appears to have been modest, and restricted to an account of a new Plesiosaur (*P. macrocephalus*) lately found at Whitby. However this specimen had perhaps been acquired overhastily by the Museum, as the following entries from the Council Minute Book show. 3rd March 1845:

'Resolved that in consequence of the Arbitrators having decided that the specimen of Plesiosaurus deposited in the Yorkshire Museum is the property of the Mar. of Normanby a memorial be presented by the Council to that Nobleman.'

31st March 1845:

'Letters having been received from Ld. Normanby respecting the Plesiosaurus reflecting upon the conduct of the Council in removing the specimen from Whitby as well as exhibiting the same at the late meeting of the British Association and Mr. Charlesworth having written an explanation of the way in which he was permitted by Mr. Liddle the lessee of the Alum Works, to remove the same, resolved that Mr. Harcourt's offer to write to Ld. Normany explaining the circumstances be gratefully accepted.'

It would appear not unreasonable for Charlesworth and the Y.P.S. Council to have assumed that Mr. Liddle, having the lease of the Alum Works, would also be the rightful owner of any fossils found with the alum. There is no further reference to this incident, but Lord Normanby did not allow the specimen to remain in the hands of the Y.P.S. Tate and Blake (1876) tentatively relate it to the specimen presented by Lord Normanby to Sir Philip Crampton, and later deposited in the Dublin Museum as *P. cramptoni*, while Simpson (1884) suggests that it is the specimen in the Whitby Museum, labelled *P. propinquus*.

Charlesworth initiated the practice in the Museum of mounting the geological specimens on small wooden boards, with a standard style of label. This made for a neat appearance in the cases, where rows and rows of fossils were neatly laid out for comparative purposes, and also proved of great benefit in later years, as the labels, pasted down onto the boards, duplicated information about the specimens from the original labels, some of which were only precariously attached to the fossils, or were written with unstable ink or in the barely legible hand of the collector.

He also experimented with the preparation and conservation of the fossils, and in 1847 could demonstrate to the members of the Society fossil sponges from the hard Flamborough chalk which he had developed from the matrix by use of dilute muriatic (hydrochloric) acid.

The railway station opened in York in 1841, and the Gardens and Museum soon became one of the City's main tourist attractions. Parties of schoolchildren came from the West Riding towns, and by March 1845 Council decided to let 'Railway Excursionists' have reduced price access to the Gardens and Museum, provided six hours notice was given. On production of the railway ticket visitors could have a ticket for the Gardens at three pence. Scholars with teachers were five shillings for the first hundred, eight shillings for two hundred, then half a crown for each further hundred. The six hours notice was required so that 'a sufficient number of the Police' could be hired to be in attendance.

The London Geological Journal

While Keeper of the Museum, Phillips had published his two volumes of the *Illustrations of the Geology of Yorkshire* with great success, much to the delight of the Society, so the literary aspirations of Charlesworth, who had already edited the *Magazine of Natural History* for three years were to be encouraged.

Charlesworth produced the first part of the short-lived *London Geological Journal* in September 1846. The editorial states the purpose of the new publication:

59

'Everyone occupied in the study of fossil remains, either as an independent subject of investigation, or in relation to Geology, must be aware that a multitude of interesting species are lying in private cabinets or public museums, comparatively lost to science, because unfigured and undescribed. The *London Geological Journal* will periodically bring to light a selection from these "medals of creation". The talent of the best draughtsmen will be employed in delineating their forms with accuracy and artistic skill, and the illustrations will be accompanied by such information as the possessors of the originals may be able and willing to supply . . .'

Charlesworth wrote at length to the Y.P.S. Council stating his intention to employ two talented pupils of the York School of Design to produce lithographs of undescribed fossils of scientific interest in Yorkshire collections:

'if the Council are willing to afford some assistance in figuring some of the more remarkable among unpublished Yorkshire fossils . . . I would undertake to place at the disposal of the Society 100 copies of the letterpress descriptive of the fossils, in return for assistance in the lithography. These memoirs as they appear in the Journal would be separately printed and paged *continuously* and in the course of time a beautifully illustrated volume would thus be formed which could be presented to other public Bodies, or exchanged for their respective publications . . .'

This the Council agreed to, offering a grant of £25 plus assistance towards the cost of lithography and the printing of the plates.

Earlier the same year Phillips had moved resolutions 'having for their object the establishment by gradual and easy means of a regular annual Publication of the transactions of the Society'. In February 1847 a publication committee was appointed, with Charlesworth as editor, and it was resolved that 'in consideration of this extra duty the Council resign their claim to the 100 copies of the Plates and Letterpress of the Yorkshire Fossils'. It seems strange that the Y.P.S. should resign all claim to the product of this arrangement, but by this time the second edition of the journal was published, and perhaps the officers realised that Charlesworth's plan was unlikely to come to fruition.

The plates issued with the journal include several by W. Bowman and W. Smith of the York School of Design; and are indeed very satisfying. The first part of the journal not unnaturally shows the support of Charlesworth's friends, and two of the articles are dated 1844, suggesting that Charlesworth had set things in motion before his appointment to York. Charlesworth stamped his personality on the publication in an editorial, in a section entitled 'Short communication, extracts and Miscellaneous Intelligence', and in a paper entitled 'On the occurrence of a species of Mosasaurus in the Chalk of England, and on the discovery of flint within the pulp-cavities of its teeth'. This innocuous-sounding subject is prefaced with

60

a long introduction with copious footnotes in which Charlesworth attacked Cuvier and Owen for their claimed ability to identify an animal from a single tooth or bone – Owen receiving the brunt of the attack – and citing several specimens originally misidentified by Owen as examples of the damage that may be done to palaeontology by hasty identification.

Charlesworth wrote that he wished:

'to claim the unfettered expression of independent opinions, and to feel that I may discuss the soundness of any Geological or Palaeontological proposition without being obnoxious to the imputation of offering frivolous or vexatious opposition to *authority*.'

The tone of his remarks must indeed have appeared obnoxious to Owen and his friends.

However, we do not have to look far to see that Charlesworth was burning with the sense of grievance over an injustice which he felt he had received at Owen's hands. One of the specimens which he cited was that of the skeleton found near Cromer which Owen initially identified as of the extinct *Anoplotherium*, but which 'has proved to be a Roebuck, with so little pretension to geological antiquity that I believe the remains have been altogether discarded . . .' Charlesworth suggested that the text of Owen's report to the B.A.A.S. meeting at Manchester had been altered in a way that was not 'consistent with perfect honesty and good faith' as Owen evidently tried to gloss over his initial misidentification of the animal.

Charlesworth continued:

'I took a great deal of trouble to prevent the committee of the Norwich Museum from exhibiting the Bacton Roebuck as an *Anoplotherium* and my doing so brought down upon me the public imputation of ignorance from Prof. Owen . . . when the Report of the proceedings at Manchester was ready for publication, the true nature of the Bacton fossil having in the meanwhile been made known, there was not the smallest necessity for retaining any allusion to its supposed Anoplotherium characters . . . the council of the British Association, by a special minute, have justified the passages as they now stand in their report, these passages being expressly written to make it appear in the *first* place that Prof. Owen did *not* originally assert the dentition of the Bacton fossil to be that of an *Anoplotherium*, and in the *second* to invest *him* with the merit of making known to the members of the Norwich Museum the worthless nature of the purchase they had been led into.'

The second number of the journal appeared in February 1847, and started with a paper contributed by Charlesworth's friend Gideon Mantell, prefaced by its covering letter, which starts:

'Sir

I hail with great pleasure the publication of the *London Geological Journal*, for the splendid contribution of undescribed fossils in the first number amply testify what a valuable medium it is likely to become for communicating and recording discoveries in Palaeontology . . .'

Charlesworth however returned to the attack on Richard Owen, and by the third issue, in May 1847, he had found a new subject for debate – the appointment of Buckland as a Trustee of the British Museum.

In his editorial Charlesworth called to mind Sir Everard Home, who, after the death of John Hunter, burnt all the manuscript catalogues of Hunter's collections and research, and quoted from the examination of Sir Henry Ellis of the Board of Trustees of the British Museum by the Parliamentary Committee, 1834:

'Do you conceive that eminent writers in the several departments of science, who have themselves advanced the bounds of knowledge, are men of system, and wedded to particular theories, and unfit on that account, from their mutual jealousies, to undertake the care of any institution of this nature?'

Although Charlesworth continues by saying that he hopes the appointment of Buckland 'May not be wholly devoid of benefit to the geological department of the Museum' he concludes by promising to revert to the subject at greater length in the future.

This must have tolled the death-knell of the journal. The sad thing is that Charlesworth's complaints were justified, and shared by others, but he took them to unacceptable lengths. Although there is no mention of the journal in the records of the Y.P.S., except that already referred to regarding the publication of illustrations, it is difficult to imagine members of the Society allowing their Curator to attack both the Trustees of the British Museum, and Dr. Buckland, one of the mentors of the infant Society in 1882 and one of its earliest Honorary Members. Had Charlesworth been able to restrain his feelings and couch his grievances in more diplomatic terms, the journal might have survived and continued to provide a forum for shorter palaeontological papers, with the Palaeontographical Society publishing the larger monographs. Thirty years later Charlesworth, writing to William Reed about some of Mantell's fossils, quoted in full a letter which Mantell had written to him some time after 1847, although it had no relevance to the subject of Charlesworth's communication. It includes the following: 'How I wish you would resume your Palaeontological Journal. Such a work is more than ever required; and if you do not soon take it up, I will start a rival publication.'

These passages have been quoted at some length, not only to illustrate the nature of the *London Geological Journal*, but also because they provide a first-hand example of Charlesworth's 'discontented disposition', with which he undoubtedly made enemies in the Yorkshire Philosophical Society.

62

The British Natural History Society

The details of this society appear to have been rather obscure, even to members of the Y.P.S. Council. It is first mentioned in the Annual Report of the Y.P.S. for 1849:

'Three associations of a scientific character, which have been formed in York during the past year, call for special notice on the part of the Council, aiming, as they do, at co-operation with this Society, though wholly supported by independent funds.'

The first two clubs were the Yorkshire Naturalists' Club and the Yorkshire Antiquarian Club. The third, the British Natural History Society:

'though not confining its investigations to this County, still, from its having originated with the Keeper of this Society's Museum, and from the benefits which it is likely to confer not only on the Yorkshire Philosophical Society, but on Natural-History generally claims, in a high degree, the support of this Society. One object of the above Society is to employ competent collectors in such districts as are known to be rich in natural productions, either recent or fossil, and to distribute the Collections, thus accumulated, amongst individuals or public institutions, who have promoted the undertaking; it being a part of the plan, that one specimen at least, of each species, shall be the property of this Society, and be deposited in this Museum, thereby securing the preservation of one complete series of all the objects that may be discovered. The Natural-History Society has commenced its labours by collecting Tertiary fossils of the Isle of Wight and adjacent cliffs of Hordwell and Barton. From these sources a vast number of valuable specimens has been obtained, more than 20,000 of which have already been distributed amongst its members.

'To this Society the Museum is indebted for an interesting series of Tertiary fossils, which forms the most valuable addition to the Geological Collection during the past year. It includes more than 50 species either new or quite unfigured in any British work; many of these are accompanied by beautiful and accurate drawings, executed, under Mr. Charlesworth's direction by Mr. Smith, an artist, whose merits as a delineater of objects of Natural-History, are well known to members of this Society.'

One would have expected Charlesworth to keep the Council and Curators informed of his activities, in view of the arrangement whereby the new Society was to deposit a complete set of specimens in the Yorkshire Museum, but there is no mention of this undertaking in the Council Minutes for 1849 or 1850. Council members evidently felt they had not been fully informed, for in March 1851 they resolved:

'That the Society having received in the last and preceeding year gifts of value from the British Natural History Society of which the executive officer is the Keeper of the Museum, that application be made to him for information as to the constitution of their Society and the relations which appear to subsist between it and the Yorkshire Philosophical Society.'

There is no record of any reply to this request in the Minute Book.

The British Natural History Society is discussed in publications by Wrigley (1944), Markham (1976) and Pyrah (1981). Wrigley refers to the project as 'Charlesworth's Illustrations', possibly a slightly confusing title considering the number of publishing ventures with which Charlesworth was associated. Wrigley describes the 'Illustrations' thus, based on specimens in the B.M.(N.H.) and the Sedgwick Museum:

'Round about 1850 Edward Charlesworth, then living at York, was the secretary and apparently the promoter of the British Natural History Society, which provided its subscribers with Hampshire Tertiary fossils obtained by paid collectors at Barton and in the Isle of Wight. This project was advertised by printed cards, dated 1849 and 1850, bearing on one side a prospectus and on the other, figures of Barton fossils lithographed by Wm. Smith of York. The same lithographer then prepared for the Society a series of excellent enlarged figures of small mollusca from Barton and the Isle of Wight, each species having two views. At present, 48 of these illustrations are known, printed in fours on twelve sheets. They were sent out singly to subscribers or purchasers, mounted on a card with a printed label of name and locality and with an actual specimen of the fossil mounted in a circular recess, the whole being covered with glass to form a paper bound slide about four inches square. Some of these illustrations were mounted on cards with name and locality labels and a small printed prospectus of the objects and subscriptions of the Society . . .'

In a footnote Wrigley adds 'Mr. Elliott [Dr. G. F. Elliot] has kindly made a search in the Museum of the Yorkshire Philosophical Society, at York (where Charlesworth once was Curator), but without result.'

Wrigley was concerned with establishing the validity or otherwise of Charlesworth's species: as he says, 'the issue to subscribers of an excellent figure, with a printed name, accompanied by an actual specimen, is surely a valid publication'. The fact that Elliott could not find any B.N.H.S. specimens at York in the 1940's is perhaps not surprising as at that period the geology collections, consisting of over 100,000 specimens, were at a very low ebb in terms of curation. However, labelled specimens did survive and are still present in the collections (for details see Pyrah, 1981).

By 1855 a subcommittee appointed to consider the position of the Curator and secretarial duties reported to Council:

'It was understood from Mr. Charlesworth that the business of the British Natural History Society had nearly come to a close, and Mr. Charlesworth engages that nothing connected with it should be carried on from the premises of the Society.'
(Council Minutes, 15th January 1855)

The B.N.H.S. appears to have remained dormant for a while, but in 1860, two years after his resignation from the Yorkshire Museum, Charlesworth, still in York, wrote to John Phillips:

'I am just making a fresh start with the illustrated sets of minute Hampshire Fossils – I have not done anything with them for some years on account of the time they take for mounting, but as I have the whole of Smith's beautiful drawings still on the stones, at an annual expense for rent, I have determined to set to work upon them again – I have thought that perhaps you would get me the Oxford Museum on the Subscription List. There is a set in the Woodwardian Museum, and I have understood that Prof. Sedgwick makes a point of calling attention to these illustrations whenever he takes his friends over the Geol. Collection.'

(O.U.M. unnumbered, 5th October 1860)

An accompanying printed brochure of the B.N.H.S. is dated 1856. It seems that the British Natural History Society was never really a success, but Charlesworth never gave up the idea or the title, for Markham records that in 1883 the B.N.H.S. was again offering Crag and Chalk specimens to subscribers; by that time Charlesworth had abandoned any idea of a museum career, and was dealing in fossils as a full-time occupation.

CHAPTER 5

The Sepoy's Friend (1854-1858)

Charlesworth's Appointment as Assistant Secretary

By 1854 the day to day handling of the affairs of the Society were becoming too onerous a task for the Honorary Secretaries, and the suggestion was made that the Society should appoint a salaried Assistant Secretary to handle the more mundane jobs. A committee chaired by John Kenrick was appointed to look into the matter, in conjunction with Charlesworth; on 15th January 1855 they reported that, for an extra £100 per year, Charlesworth was willing to undertake all the duties of the Clerk and the Secretary, except for the collection of subscriptions, and in addition would give a course of lectures on the Natural History contents of the Museum. After discussion and objections to this plan the committee was requested to make a further report, which they submitted on 29th January:

'We are of the opinion that the circumstances of the Society have become such as to render it very important that the Society should have a paid officer generally on the premises. We find also this necessity is felt and urged by a large number of members of the Society not being members of the Council.

'We believe that in many respects Mr. Charlesworth's situation in connextion with the Society would enable him to be more useful than anyone else in this position.

'But we fear that the state of the Society's finances is such as to render the amount of salary already proposed inexpedient.

'We suggest an intermediate course might be adopted by way of experiment, viz. that the Society should offer to Mr. Charlesworth the sum of £50, he undertaking the office of assistant secretary for one year; on the understanding that the salary will cease at the close of the year, if the increase in the funds of the Society is not sufficient to justify its continuance.

'If this proposal is adopted, Mr. Kenrick and Mr. Allis have, though reluctantly, signified their willingness to be proposed as honorary secretaries for the following year; and we think it important that they should be appointed . . .'

Kenrick then wrote to Phillips with details of the new arrangements; it seems that not all Council members were happy with the idea of giving Charlesworth this additional responsibility and salary:

'I do not know whether you have heard anything lately about the affairs of the Y.P.S. It has been passing through a sort of crisis, which may be said only to have terminated yesterday. The sudden departure of Travis left us in considerable perplexity about the secretariat, from which we were temporarily relieved by Hay and Allis. But as they declared against holding their office longer than till the annual Meeting, we had to consider of some permanent arrangement. No one was willing to undertake the office and there was indeed a general feeling in the Council that the duties of a Secretary had so much increased,. that it was too much to expect an individual to undertake without some remuneration. A resolution was therefore past [sic] that it was expedient to have a paid Secretary, which was followed by an instruction to a special Committee to enquire of Mr. Charlesworth, if he would undertake the duty, with the addition of Peacock's (except collecting) for £100 additional. He was very ready to do so. Before anything further had passed with him Mr. V. Harcourt, who had not been present at any of the meetings, expressed his most decided disapprobation of it, and at a Council to which he came, the matter was deferred for a week to see what could be done. At that meeting several members said the arrangement was not satisfactory to them, but as no one would take the office, they were driven to it as a matter of necessity. Mr. V. Harcourt had previously intimated to me, through Mr. Hay, his wish that I would offer my services, but that was impossible, as long as it seemed that nothing stood between Charlesworth and £250 a year, provided only no one presented himself to take the office. But after the declaration of Mr. Harcourt's strong opinion and the partial dissatisfaction of others, it seemed to me very undesirable that the Society should be driven to a step they did not approve, merely because they had no alternative. I went over therefore the following day to Osbaldwick to see if I could persuade Allis to join me in offering our services for a time at least, so that no irrevocable step should be taken and I succeeded. When the Council met again a new fact came out – the accounts showed a deficiency of £12.15 and the crippling of all the other departments by spending £100 a year more on a Secretary was strongly argued against it. The upshot has been that Charlesworth had been appointed paid assistant Secretary with £50 additional, taking the Clerk's duty and engaging to attend 6 *continuous* hours 6 days a week – but as an experiment; while, also as an experiment for the same period of 12 months, Allis and I have been appointed Hon. Secs.'

Kenrick then alludes to the concern felt by the Society over falling membership and attendances at the morning meetings:

'The public dissatisfaction has led to the abolition of the printed orders, and the extension of the privilege of bringing in visitors, to member's *wives* . . . I fear that if we do not provide something solid in the mornings, we shall be given up to flashy *evening* lectures . . .' (O.U.M. 1855/4, 7th February 1855)

Charlesworth now applied himself to the problem of falling membership, and in July 1855 submitted to the Council a printed circular, drawing attention to the need for more county members and suggesting changes in the subscription rates to encourage them:

'It is earnestly to be hoped that an Institution which may now be said to enjoy an European celebrity, and which among English Provincial Scientific Associations stands alone, may not henceforth have to feel that it is supported only because its grounds form an agreeable promenade for the Citizens of York . . .'

The first half of this sentence may be explained as an example of the flattering style in which Charlesworth was inclined to write, but in the second half he places his finger on what was to prove a basic factor in the existence of the Y.P.S. over the ensuing 100 years – namely that a key to the Gardens, which were the only such facility in the centre of York, and formed the quickest and most pleasant route from the residential area of Marygate to the heart of the City, proved to be a major attraction of Society membership (pl. 7).

His work for the Society as Secretary must have been satisfactory as the Council meeting of January 1856 resolved to continue his services on the same terms as before, and by January 1857 the Council could resolve:

'That the success of the financial arrangement and the ability and zeal of Mr. Charlesworth justify the Council in making his salary Two hundred and fifty pounds . . .'

Robert Davies reported to John Phillips that:

'In our museum, at the annual meeting last Tuesday, there was a flash of liberality – Mr. Harcourt lauded the increase of Charlesworth's salary – perhaps because it was supported by one of his own order – He who runs may read – a vile pun! [This may refer to William Rudston Read]' (O.U.M. 1857/-, 7th February 1857)

One example of Charlesworth's ability as Secretary was the engaging of Mr. Waterhouse Hawkins to give a lecture in February 1856, on extinct animals. Benjamin Waterhouse Hawkins was the wild-life artist and sculptor who, working with Richard Owen, recreated for the Crystal Palace site at Sydenham life-sized models of dinosaurs and other prehistoric animals, in 1852-4.

Hawkins returned in November of the same year to give two lectures on the 'Natural History of the Ancient and present world'. Tickets for these lectures sold so well that the Society had to arrange for each lecture to be given twice. Some idea of the tone of the lectures can be gained from a letter from Hawkins to Charlesworth in October 1856:

'but I prefer myself to be a missionary to propagate a popular acquaintance with Natural History by placing visibly or graphically before my audience such facts and instances of animal life both extinct and recent as may tempt, at least the rising generation, to give their attention to the subject on the grounds of its educational value and its intimate connection with everyday life.'

Pl. 7.   The Museum Gardens. A mid-19th century view by H. Cave. The fountain to the right can now be seen in the grounds of Fairfax House, Castlegate

An entry in the Council Minute for 16th February 1857, throws an interesting light on the problems of servicing the Museum's collections:

'In reference to the re-arrangement of the Geological Collection the Curator explained to the Council that Mr. Kitching had undertaken to have labels printed at the Retreat [an institution for the mentally ill under the enlightened management of the Quakers] free of cost to the Society in exchange for duplicate specimens, but that a delay had arisen in consequence of the Patient who acts as Printer to the Institution being temporarily disqualified from going on with the work.'

Charlesworth was finding it difficult to cope with the demands of the Museum alone, as there is little evidence that the Honorary Curators were willing to give much assistance with the physical tasks of curating, and the Sub-Curator, Henry Baines, was also responsible for the Gardens and the various activities which they were used for. Charlesworth may also have been in financial difficulty, as we shall see.

In fact, concern was growing nationally for the situation of museum curators and other scientists, many of whom found themselves in a position of considerable responsibility with poor financial rewards and often a lowly status in the museum hierarchy of Honorary Curators, officers and Trustees.

In 1856 the Parliamentary Committee to the B.A.A.S. had reported on 'whether any measures could be adopted by Government or Parliament that would improve the position of Science or its Cultivators in this Country'. Sir Charles Lyell had suggested to the committee that:

'five or six towns should first be selected, which have exhibited their taste for scientific knowledge by the foundation of museums and the appointment of curators, such as York and Bristol. The Government might enter into an arrangement with the latter to double their salaries, so as to secure to them a continuation of the local patronage already afforded to them and prevent the new grant from becoming merely a substitute for it.'

This was brought to the attention of the Y.P.S. members at the A.G.M. in the spring of 1857 by Rudston Read, who made an eloquent plea for a larger salary and higher status for Charlesworth, which met with agreement by Vernon Harcourt.

Charlesworth wrote to the Council on 2nd March 1857:

'Dear Sir,

The encouragement to take up Natural history as a livelihood is now so very much greater than it was a few years back that I think it possible I might be able to obtain one or perhaps two Pupils with a view to qualify them for entering upon the pursuit as a Profession, provided the Council are willing that in return for work done in the Museum they should enjoy the advantages under proper regulations of the use

70

of the library, access to the Collections & c. Such an arrangement would I think in a great degree obviate what hitherto has proved a serious impediment to keeping the Collections in a creditable state and that is the absence of a curator's assistant, when in a variety of ways manual aid is so frequently needed by this officer in the discharge of his duties. As an example in point, I may mention that the whole of the skeletons, Birds, Reptiles and fishes are inaccessible to the Curator from the nature of the cases in which they are placed, unless he has the help of a second person to enable him to get at them. The assistance that can be obtained by calling on one of the Garden laborers or the Subcurator by no means meets the difficulty, because the occasion in which the presence of a second party in the Museum is needed are of almost hourly occurrence. Our valuable collection of Plants and Insects are now almost lost sight of because the shewing them to visitors would involve so large an amount of time as to almost prohibit the Curator from voluntarily bringing them into notice, but this objection would be entirely removed if the Curator had an assistant. I need hardly say that I should be most cautious not to take any Youth in the Capacity of a Pupil without his shewing a natural taste for the study, and upon general grounds there being a reasonable probability both in relation to my own credit and the interests of the Museum of the experiment proving successful – the condition would also probably be considered imperative by the Council should they consent to the arrangement, and that is that the responsibility should rest entirely upon myself and the Guardians of the Pupil, and the Society not to be mixed up with it in any way.'

At the Council meeting of March 1857 it was agreed unanimously that Charlesworth should be allowed to take pupils upon this basis, but I have found no record of this being taken up. Nor does it seem that there was any discussion in Council about improving his salary or status – perhaps they were hoping that Parliament might take up Lyell's suggestion of grant-aid to museums.

Charlesworth had obviously earned the approval of senior members of the Society and of the B.A.A.S., and no doubt was looking forward to the future with a feeling of satisfaction, unaware of the pitfall that fate was preparing for him.

On 16th September 1857 a meeting was held in the York Guildhall to promote a subscription for the relief of the sufferers of the Indian Mutiny. The rebellion during the summer had been sparked off by the use of lard to grease the cartridges which were issued to the armed forces in India by the British administration, this entailing the handling of animal fat which was contrary to the religious edicts of their faith; the deeper roots of the uprising lay in the recent annexation by the British of the kingdom of Oude. Not only did the massacre of British soldiers and civilians leave many dependants, both in India and back home, destitute, but the stories which filtered back to England of the atrocities committed by the Sepoys against women and children not unnaturally raised a cry for vengeance against what was seen as a sub-human enemy. The call was for a Christian justice which would avenge every drop of British blood spilt upon the sub-continent, that would summarily put to death every Indian who may have had a hand in the uprising, and would raze the city of Delhi to the ground, not a stone to be left standing. A few people argued for moderation, and it was evidently privately admitted in some circles that the behaviour of the British in India had been faulty; that the missionaries in their attempts to convert the population to Christianity had succeeded only in destroying the basis of religious stability in the area, and that the Bible which we preached to the natives showed a religion every bit as blood-thirsty as their own.

The meeting at York was convened by the Lord Mayor to initiate a subscription for the Indian Relief Fund, and was addressed by William Vernon Harcourt who, moving the first resolution, called that:

'our soldiers go forward, armed as the ministers of justice – as ministers, in point of fact, he would not say of a righteous retribution, but of a righteous attempt to re-establish peace, and order, and security, and just administration of law.'

He was followed by Alderman Meek, who mentioned the treachery of the Sepoys, and by the Rev. Canon Baillie, who asked those present:

'to ponder well whether our government of India had been hitherto always conducted upon principles of equity and true justice . . .'

Such a moment of national rage and sorrow was bound to offer pitfalls for the unwary, and Charlesworth, with his family background of ministering Christianity, and geologist's view of the accuracy of the Bible as a literal record of God's views on earthly subjects, waded straight in. Quoting from an article published by the *Yorkshireman* the previous month, which started 'The races of India must be taught what it is to provoke the might of England . . . and who shall say what shall be the limit to our revenge . . .' he went on to point out how an intelligent Indian could quote the Christian Scriptures taken to them by the missionaries, as containing examples of hideous atrocities committed in the name of God. After loud protestations from the meeting against this apparent attack on the Holy Scripture, Charlesworth was allowed to reply that he had not intended to suggest that anything in the Scriptures justified the Sepoy's conduct, but Mr. Watts, author of the offending article, then stated that his views had been grossly distorted and caricatured, that he believed in revenge, not retaliation (!), and that, having spent 15 years in India, he could affirm that Mr. Charlesworth's 'hypothetical intelligent Sepoy' did not exist. Further speakers called the meeting back onto the subject of a subscription fund, and almost £300 was raised. (Reported in detail in the *Yorkshireman*, *Yorkshire Gazette* and *York Herald*, all for 19th September 1857.) However, in Mr. Watts of the *Yorkshireman* Charlesworth had found an opponent who perhaps shared with him some excesses of character, for that paper published a long article attacking him in scathing terms, from which the following are only excerpts:

'The Sepoy's Friend.

The Yorkshire Philosophical Society's Museum is fortunate, above all other Museums, in that it possesses a curator among its curiosities. Of all the wonders preserved in the classic halls of WILKINS – of all the things placed under glass or painfully mounted on wire – not the big antediluvian lizard, the choicest among the Roman pots, or the monster lily of Mr. Baines, is half so rare a specimen – so great a curiosity, as the learned curator himself, Mr. Charlesworth.

'The most charitable conclusion we can arrive at is that Mr. Charlesworth did not mean what he said – that much study of saurians had distracted his wits – that mollusks had settled on his brain and moths had driven him mad . . .

'Let the Curator ponder on it with half the diligence he has bestowed on the habits of shell-fish, and we wager a dinotherium to a dead caterpillar that he renounces his very peculiar views on the treatment of mutineers – those views which make him the greatest curiosity in the Yorkshire Philosophical Society's Museum.

'We trust it may not be thought that we have devoted too much space to the Curator and his eccentricities. But it is not only a question between the *Yorkshireman* and Mr. Charlesworth. The question as to whether the mutinous sepoys should or should not be adequately punished is of great and universal concernment. And we are content to know that, with a few miserable exceptions – howling Irish priests, rabid peace-and-cotton men, museum-curators and such cattle – the sepoy has no friends in England. For Mr. Charlesworth, we commend him to the serious attention of his patrons, the Philosophers – custodiant ipsum custodem – let the curator be cared for.

'Since writing the above our doubts of the curator's sanity have been more than confirmed. It is clear, not only that Mr. Charlesworth is incapable of any effort of reasoning, but that he cannot even make a statement with accuracy. With the pertinacity peculiar to persons in his condition, the unhappy gentleman, not content with the exhibition he has already made, sends us a printed paper, wherein the charges against us are repeated in a still wilder and more incoherent manner than on Wednesday. We are accused of suggesting "indiscriminate slaughter in unmistakeable terms" – although in the same breath a passage is quoted wherein we expressly discriminate those who have "embrued their hands in British blood" as fit objects of punishment.

'Familiar as we are with imbecility under all its aspects, we feel that this is a subject beyond our experience. The friends of Mr. Charlesworth may not know that there is a public establishment down Bootham way, especially devoted to the treatment of such cases.'

It is probable that many of Charlesworth's friends and colleagues at the Museum would have agreed with him in private as to the injustice of advocating butchery of every Sepoy on the grounds of vengeance, but the climate of public opinion was evidently such that it was not wise in public to go much further than Harcourt's call for 'a righteous attempt to re-establish peace'.

All three York newspapers had, inevitably, linked Mr. Charlesworth with the Y.P.S., and reminded their readers that a man *in his position* should not have misused it so. Perhaps Mr. Watts now began to cool down, for in the *Yorkshireman* of 3rd October appeared a letter to the editor from 'No friend of the Sepoy' regretting Charlesworth's remarks but suggesting that the *Yorkshireman* may have been a little too severe on him and hoping that the incident did not lead to his dismissal from his post. On the same page the editor, after acknowledging this letter, and pointing out that Mr. Charlesworth's remarks were, to say the least 'indiscreet, ill-timed, ill-judged and curiously inconsequential' assured his readers that:

'We sincerely join in the hope of our correspondent, that the Curator's late indiscretion may not be followed by any untoward consequences to himself. We are willing to admit the value of Mr. Charlesworth's services in his own appointed sphere, and should be very sorry indeed were we to be deprived of his talents in that capacity in which he has become so eminent.'

The only concern of the newspaper was, not Charlesworth's own theological views, but his duty not to impose them on others:

'We now take leave of this subject, trusting that, whatever steps the Philosophical Society may feel called upon to take, they will not involve the retirement of the Curator, to whose scientific attainment and to whose valuable services we cheerfully bear testimony.'

Two days later Charlesworth wrote to the Council of the Y.P.S., explaining that, in his unpremeditated speech calling for humane and merciful action, he had not intended to offend the religious feelings of the meeting. He continued:

'While wishing to claim that liberty of conscience in matters of belief, which is consistent with the spirit of the age in regard to religious toleration, I fully understand the position in which the Council is placed, in respect to the general body of the subscribers, and the injury which might arise to the Society, if it was supposed that I take advantage of the opportunities which my post affords, to promulgate opinions calculated to lessen reverence for the authority of the Scriptures. That I am not open to this imputation is, I think, proved by the success which has attended my efforts to add to the Society's prosperity, by increasing the number of its members – a result largely depending upon the exercise of personal influence.

74

'At the same time I fully see the necessity, after what has now occurred, of carefully abstaining from anything which, either by misconstruction or otherwise, might create discord and I willingly give you a pledge to that effect.

'I am also ready to resign my post, if it appear to the Council to be for the interests of the Society, that I should do so though it may be easily supposed that in its present career of prosperity, with which the Council have honourably and publicly connected my name, I should take this step with extreme regret.'

The Council then resolved that Charlesworth be required to 'enter into an agreement that he will not, either in public or in private, use any expressions tending to disparage the authority of the Holy Scriptures, or calculated to injure the Society in the opinion of the Christian public'; this agreement was to be signed, printed and circulated to all the members. However, by the next week letters had been received from Kenrick to William Vernon Harcourt, and from John Phillips to the Rev. Canon Hey, recommending that the latter proposal be reconsidered, and it was agreed by those present that, having obtained Charlesworth's signature to the agreement it should merely be entered in the Minutes.

Bearing in mind the contemporary state of geological and biological science, with the publication of Darwin's *The Origin of Species* only a few months away, Charlesworth's promise not to 'either in public or in private use any expressions tending to disparage the authority of the Holy Scripture . . .' would have been difficult to maintain to the satisfaction of the more staid Society members.

By November Kenrick was writing to Phillips:

'There have been rumours of a movement among certain zealous people, against Charlesworth, notwithstanding the explanations and promises which he made to the Council. Dr. Shann, Whytehead, D. Russell, H. A. Champney are mentioned as promoters. That they have been endeavouring to get up a memorial to the Council to dismiss him is certain; but I believe they have met with so little success that it will never come before us. There was a large muster at the last Council meeting in the expectation of its being presented.'   (O.U.M. 1857/-, 16th November 1857)

Kenrick's optimism proved mistaken, and at a Special Council meeting on 16th January 1858 Charlesworth resigned his post.

'A memorial was read from certain members of the Society relating to Mr. Charlesworth, and also the following letter from himself:–

"After a careful consideration of my present position, in relation to the circumstances which have arisen within the last few months, I feel that it may be for the interests of the Society and myself that I should place my Resignation in your hands; and I hereby do so."

'Whereupon it was resolved:
1. That Mr. Charlesworth's resignation be accepted and that he be requested to

continue his services to the end of the present Quarter – March 31, when in acknowledgment of the zeal with which he has promoted the interests of the Society and his valuable services in increasing its funds and augmenting its Collections, he shall receive the whole year's salary, namely Two Hundred and Fifty pounds.
2. That Mr. Charlesworth's resignation be communicated to the Memorialists through the medium of Dr. Shann.'

Charlesworth, however, left the Museum within two weeks; and on 6th February the Secretaries asked Council for assistance in the investigation of Charlesworth's accounts, for which they were joined by Mr. Rudston Read, J. Meek Jnr and T. S. Noble. A search in the Society's present offices has failed to discover the account books for the period, and the Council Minutes give no details, but the next entry in the Council Minute book suggests that upwards of £300 was missing.

'It was resolved that authority be given to the Treasurer and Secretaries to negotiate with Mr. Charlesworth for the delivery to him of his fossils now in the possession of the Society, on his making good the sum which may appear to be owing to the Society, after allowing him the current year's salary.'

By 1st March the Treasurer could report that Charlesworth's father had agreed to make good the deficiency in his son's accounts, and by the end of March Charlesworth had sorted out his own specimens from recent donations to the Society, with the assistance (or supervision) of Rudston Read, William Reed, the Rev. Henry Short and William Proctor. Proctor, who was the Hon. Curator of Geology and Mineralogy, together with William Reed, with Charlesworth's help, then checked that all the specimens donated to the Museum during the previous 10 years were present in the collections, and reported to the Council that all was in order. Despite this assurance rumours began to circulate that Charlesworth 'had appropriated specimens from the Society's Collections, and had thrown obstacles in the way of an investigation'; at Charlesworth's request the Council instructed the Secretary to write to him 'expressing the conviction of the Council that there was no ground for the rumour referred to.'

This was not only the end of Charlesworth's formal association with the Yorkshire Museum; it also marked the end of his ambition as a professional museum curator, and he turned to dealing in fossils as his main employment. His skills as a curator were still in demand among private collectors, – in 1860 he wrote to Phillips 'It is not unlikely that I may be at Manchester within the next few days, for some of the private collectors there want me to assist them in getting their Cabinets into order before the meeting there of the Association' (O.U.M. unnumbered, 5th October 1860); he attempted to revive the British Natural History Society, and while he remained in York his contacts with the Philosophical Society were apparently cordial. On 1st April 1861 Council agreed that he could borrow more books than the rules permitted, on the grounds of scientific research, and the Council also purchased specimens from him. After he moved to London, Charlesworth continued to show a suprising degree of loyalty to the Yorkshire Museum.

All this suggests that Charlesworth's parting from the Yorkshire Museum was not as bitter as might be supposed. His skill in curating the collection and in promoting the interests of the Society were acknowledged, even by his enemies. However the deficiency in the accounts was caused, it seems there must have been some explanation or exonerating circumstances as the Society would hardly have accepted his application for membership, as they did, soon after his resignation if they found he had deliberately and dishonestly defrauded them of several hundred pounds. His friends, Phillips, Kenrick, Rudston Read were senior members of the Council while none of the memorialists were Council members or Honorary Curators. It seems probable that if he had chosen to fight for his job he might have succeeded, but after 14 years at the Museum, at the age of 45 Charlesworth might have not been unwilling to leave. The salary at the Museum was evidently inadequate for his needs, and the duties left no time for research or other projects.

The Yorkshire Geological Society

The formation, during the late 1830's and 1840's, of local specialist clubs had a considerable impact on the activities of the Yorkshire Philosophical Society. The York-based societies were formed, at least partly, as offshoots of the Society, and worked with it in a spirit of co-operation, but one West Riding society provided vigorous competition.

The Geological Society of the West Riding of Yorkshire was founded in December 1837, at a meeting of coal and iron-masters at Wakefield. John Phillips assisted at subsequent meetings, at which the aims of the society were formulated, and its name was changed to include the polytechnic interest. Not until 1876 did the society formally widen its field of interest to the whole county. A full account of its early history is given in J. W. Davis' *History of the Yorkshire Geological and Polytechnic Society* (1889).

The society confined itself to geological (including prehistoric archae-ological) and mining engineering subjects, at first within the West Riding of Yorkshire. This specialised forum attracted papers for publication in their Proceedings, which was eventually to grow into one of the country's leading geological journals.

Within a couple of years of the formation of the West Riding society its effects were being felt in York. In 1841 Goldie wrote to Phillips:

'The success of the West Riding Society I learn is certainly ascribed to the energy of its Secy., Wilson of Barnsley. They seem to have taken to themselves all the work wch. Harcourt in his early report cut out for us, & *we* are at this moment little more than proprietors of an excellent Museum.'　　　　　(O.U.M. 1841 62.a.2)

By the end of the decade Phillips, Charlesworth and Kenrick had all submitted papers for publication by the West Riding society rather than that at York.

Analysis of the Yorkshire Philosophical Society's publications shows how complete was the take-over of geological publication in the county by the geological society. In the 1850's only four geological papers were published by the Society, and, in the period 1847-1874, of a total of 444 papers, only 80 are geological. This is in complete contrast to the early years, when, of 110 papers presented to the Society between 1823-1830, 79 were geological. In addition, these first 79 papers cover a wide range of geological enquiry throughout the county, while the 80 papers published by the Society after 1847 are mostly related to specimens in the Yorkshire Museums's collections.

Although the West Riding geologists succeeded in becoming the county's major geological publishers, they were not so successful with their museum. Not only was this in competition with the already well-established museums of the various Yorkshire literary and philosophical institutions, but the society itself led a peripatetic existence, with its officers spread throughout the West Riding towns, and meetings held in different venues; the ownership of a museum under these circumstances was something of an anachronism. In 1841 a suggestion was made that the geological society should be amalgamated with the York-based Yorkshire Agricultural Society, the museums of the two societies to be combined at York. This plan was rejected, but in 1843 the Secretary, J. Travis Clay, wrote 'The museum at Wakefield appears to me to be nearly a useless expense, no one can visit it, and it creates no interest in favour of the Society'; the next year the contents were transferred to the Museum of the Leeds Philosophical and Literary Society.

Early in 1842 the Yorkshire Philosophical Society sent a letter to various institutions, including the Yorkshire Geological Society, asking them to join in inviting the British Association to York in 1843. Thomas Wilson, the Secretary of the Y.G.S., wrote to his colleague Mr. Embleton, informing him of the circular and continuing:

'I have suggested that if the object is merely, by a loan of the share of honour, to draw from us a portion of the money to be spent in York, it is not worth while to stir in the

78

matter, but that if there be a disposition to form a permanent union of the Philosophical Societies, for mutual advice, assistance and improvement, it would be as well to enter into a consideration of the question . . .'

Wilson wrote back to the Yorkshire Philosophical Society that his society:

'would indeed suggest to the Y.P.S. as the leading Institution, the desirableness of forming a permanent union of the Lity. and Philal. Societies of the County and of establishing an Annual Meeting on the plan that has been adopted by the Mechanics Institutes and has in their case been found so beneficial – by reviving the energies of their Conductors and by bringing under their notice plans that in other places had been found productive of advantage. It cannot be denied that most of the provincial Soctys. are powerless to advance the bounds of Science or even to communicate what is already known and that they would cease altogether to exist in many places, except for the desire of preserving their collections . . . Were efficient and permanent union of this kind established, so that the separate Societies would really consider themselves part of a whole they might then see no impropriety in voting a portion of their fund for what would then be a common object.'

Such a union might have filled the communication gap left by the demise of the system of extended lecture tours by itinerant lecturers, but the tone of Wilson's letter was possibly rather too direct for the York philosophers. A sub-committee was formed, consisting of Goldie, who as we have seen was concerned about the geologists' activities, Phillips, who was complaining about the pressure of work due to his London and British Association commitments, Vernon Harcourt, for whom the founding of the British Association 10 years earlier was to have been the means of uniting the provincial societies, and Wellbeloved, now in his 70's. There is no further report in the Council minutes from this committee. The idea of such a union hung on until the mid-1860's, with little success, although a meeting of delegates from the philosophical societies of Yorkshire was held in the Yorkshire Museum in April 1859.

Other Local Societies

Soon after the formation of the Yorkshire Geological Society the York philosophers saw the birth, in 1842, of the York Archaeological Society (later to add Yorkshire Architectural to its title and become known as the Y.A.Y.A.S.) which studied the architecture of mediaeval churches; the Yorkshire Antiquarian Club, formed in 1849 to excavate archaeological sites, the finds to be donated to the Yorkshire Museum, and the Yorkshire Naturalists' Club, formed in the same year, to hold meetings, exhibit specimens and collect funds for the purchase of specimens for Museums in the county, especially the Yorkshire Museum. The latter club was short-lived; the York and District Field Naturalists' Society succeeded it in 1874.

The archaeologists in particular found the Proceedings of the Yorkshire Philosophical Society a useful vehicle for their communications, and from 1847 onwards, the majority of papers published by the Society have been archaeological.

However, while the presence of archaeological clubs strengthened the Society's publishing venture, the activities of these specialist groups had an adverse effect on the general meetings of the Society. Local researchers preferred to give their talks to the specialist audience rather than to a general meeting, and the Society lost the scientific communications which had formed the mainstay of its early years; after 1845 the term 'scientific communications' was dropped from the Annual Report.

CHAPTER 6

Palaeontological Wealth (1857-1892)

WHEN EDWARD CHARLESWORTH RESIGNED FROM THE post of Keeper in January 1858 the Council appointed Mr. Charles Wakefield as a temporary measure while they sought a new Keeper. Although on this occasion Mr. Wakefield was only employed for some six months, at a later date he was to serve as Keeper of the Museum for about 15 years, so the following brief biography has been compiled from material preserved in J. A. Knowles' manuscript scrapbook *York Artists* Vol. II, No. 380.

Charles Wakefield (1834-1919)

Charles Wakefield was born in York in 1834. He was educated privately, then attended the York School of Art. Leaving the school he devoted his ability to the practice of teaching drawing and that of natural history. He was appointed drawing master at the newly founded Primitive Methodist Elmfield College in 1864, and at the same time was drawing master at Bootham School. When the College became a limited company he was elected Chairman of the Board of Governors. He later became interested in numismatics and was Honorary Curator of Numismatics, and a Vice-President of the Yorkshire Philosophical Society; after his death in 1919 his own collection was sold at Sotheby's. Wakefield lived at Heslington House just outside York; he bequeathed £50,000 to the York Blind School, and Heslington House and its lands to York Corporation. Of his character his obituary in the *Yorkshire Gazette* states:

'He was one of the most methodical of men, and it is on record that many at the school found it not a little difficult to conform to his wishes in this respect . . . He spent a great deal of his time among the volumes [of the York Subscription Library] being of a most studious nature. Mr. Wakefield, who was a bachelor, had a striking personality, and impressed one in a manner which made him not easily forgotten. He prided himself upon his thrift, to which he attributed no small amount of his success.'

The Council applied themselves to the task of finding another Keeper with a sense of urgency, because they had just completed an extension to the Museum which added three more galleries to the display area. In February 1857 Robert Davies had written to Phillips:

'In today's newspaper there is a letter, signed "Wm. [Rudston] Read" suggesting an enlargement of the Museum, posteriorly. Thus providing a place for the pavements (Roman tesselated pavements) and making more room for ye. collections – Is not this the notion you once had? But after all the L.S.D. is the difficulty.'

(O.U.M. 1857/-, 14th February 1857)

In April of that year the attention of the Society was drawn by Allis to the recent discovery of a large ichthyosaur, some 25ft in length, in the alum-pits at Whitby. Phillips agreed that the Museum should try to secure the specimen and a subscription was begun for its purchase, but the donation by the Rev. Danson Richardson Roundell of the £110 necessary for its purchase made this unnecessary, and no doubt relieved Charlesworth, who had taken upon himself the risk of the purchase, in order to ensure the specimen for the Museum. The addition of this giant fossil to the already overcrowded galleries of the Museum made the provision of additional space essential, and under Wm. Rudston Read's energetic campaigning an appeal was launched for £1,000, of which £876 was subscribed within the year. By November of 1857 John Kenrick was able to tell Phillips that the new building was proceeding well, although some money was still needed; raising it was proving difficult because some Y.P.S. members were:

'busy in bricks and mortar on their own account – Mr. Anderson in enlarging his dining room, Mr. Hudson [the railway magnate] is erecting his Byzantine castle at Ouse Cliff . . .'   (O.U.M. 1857/-, 16th November 1857)

This extension to the Museum building filled in the space between the Museum and the King's Manor, and provided three new galleries, the centre one of which would provide space for the three large saurians in the Society's possession.

By 6th February 1858, three weeks after Charlesworth's resignation, three applications for the vacant post had been received, from Prof. Morris, Mr. Lycett and Mr. Dallas; these applications indicate the high regard with which the scientific world by then viewed the collections at York. John Morris (1810-1866) published, in 1845, a *Catalogue of British Fossils* which became the main reference catalogue for British material; in 1855 he was appointed to the post of Professor of Geology at University College London. John Lycett (1804-1882) had specialised in the study of Jurassic palaeontology, and had co-authored, with Morris, the Palaeontographical Society's Monograph on the Great Oolite Mollusca of Minchinhampton, which was published 1850-1855. William Sweetland Dallas (1824-1890) was at the time best known as an entomologist. In addition to numerous papers on entomological subjects he had contributed 28 chapters on zoology to Orr's *Circle of the Sciences*, which were reprinted as a separate work, *A Natural History of the Animal Kingdom* in 1856. The Council decided to defer an appointment and offer Professor Morris £50 to visit the Museum and arrange and label the geological specimens during the Easter vacation. However Morris had second thoughts about coming to York – one can hardly imagine the salary or facilities here would have been worth the sacrifice of a Chair at University College – and his withdrawal from the candidature was announced to the Society in a letter from Sir Roderick Murchison. During the spring applications were also received from Mr. Oldham, Dr. T. Spencer Cobbold and Professor Sedgwick's assistant at Cambridge, Lucas Barrett. At the Council meeting of 7th June Dallas was elected to the post.

William Sweetland Dallas (1824-1890)

W. S. Dallas was born in London in 1824, and from an early age became interested in natural history and especially entomology. When he was still a child his father's business ventures failed and both his elder brothers had to abandon their studies and enter business life in the City. When William left school he found this life distasteful, and fortunately the family fortunes seem to have recovered sufficiently by then for him to take up natural history as a profession, studying in the British Library Reading Room. His mentor in the field of entomology was Dr. John Edward Gray of the British Museum, and he contributed original papers to the Entomological Society from 1847 until 1853. He was elected a Fellow of the Linnaean Society in 1849; from 1850 to 1852 he was engaged in cataloguing the Hemipterous insects in the B.M. and arranged the natural history collections in the Crystal Palace. Throughout his life he improved on his knowledge of languages, which included as well as French, German and Italian, a knowledge of Danish, Swedish and Norwegian.

When appointed by the Yorkshire Philosophical Society to succeed Charlesworth in 1858 there were many points of similarity between the 34 year old Dallas and Charlesworth at the age of 31, when he had been appointed to the same post in 1844. Both were acknowledged to be industrious and capable in the curation of museum collections, with experience at the British Museum. Both had a childhood interest in natural history; both had publishing experience and an interest in scientific journalism. However, in contrast to Charlesworth, Dallas, married with four children, was of a retiring character, and obtained the warm friendship of many older naturalists, including Charles Darwin, Charles Lyell and

Thomas Huxley. This fortunate character must have been one of the features which enabled him to succeed where Charlesworth had struggled, and it could be said that Dallas had the career which Charlesworth wished for, as when he left the employment of the Yorkshire Philosophical Society, he obtained the post of Assistant Secretary to the Geological Society, which he held for 21 years, during which period he also edited the *Annals and Magazine of Natural History* which incorporated *The Magazine of Natural History* which Charlesworth had earlier edited for three years. While at York Dallas wrote for the *Westminster Review* and prepared translations of papers for the *Annals* and the *Philosophical Magazine*, as well as working on the *Zoological Record*. He was Honorary Secretary of the Yorkshire Naturalists' Club for 10 years from 1859, and each summer gave a course of lectures at the summer school at Alnwick maintained by the Duke of Northumberland. Woodward wrote:

'In taking a retrospect of Mr. W. S. Dallas' useful but arduous career, one is astonished at the vast amount of important work achieved by him and the small share of recognition which it fell to his lot to receive. But a glance at the nature of that work will suffice to show that by far the largest and most laborious part was occupied by him either as a Curator, an Editor, a Journalist, or as a Translator, in all of which capacities – however well the duties may have been performed – the *kudos* is but small.'

As Dallas was, at the time of his appointment to the Yorkshire Museum, inexperienced in the curation of fossil material, arrangements were made for Samuel Pickworth Woodward, of the British Museum, to report on the geological collections, at Vernon Harcourt's suggestion, with Mr. Dallas to accompany him at the Society's expense. They found that the number of geological specimens on display was 8,181, and mentioned areas of particular deficiency, e.g. Devonian corals, Carboniferous fish palates, and some Jurassic beds of Southern England, in the hope that members might have been able to fill the gaps in the collections. Unfortunately the full text of this report does not seem to have survived.

During the summer of 1858 the three large saurians which were to form the main display in the building extension were studied and named by Professor Owen and conserved by Mr. Dew of the British Museum. These three specimens were to be exhibited in the long central room of the extension, two mounted on the wall 'in conformity with the practice of the British Museum' and protected by a screen of glass, the third, the 20ft long plesiosaur, to be placed in a horizontal case. On each side of this long gallery is a small square gallery. That linking the geology gallery with the new 'Saurian Room' was to house a collection of Yorkshire fossils which was maintained separately from the general collection; the other was to take the collection of British birds. Evidently concern was felt about the humidity surrounding the large saurians, for by April 1859 it was resolved that apertures were to be made in the large glass case for ventilation, and at some later date – it is not known when – the glass screen in front of the wall mounted specimens was removed. (Pl. 8.)

William Bean's Collection

No sooner was the new Yorkshire Geology Room brought into use than one of the major Yorkshire geological collections came onto the market; that of William Bean of Scarborough. A member of a family of naturalists whose fortunes have been chronicled by McMillan and Greenwood (1972), William Bean's father, also William (fl. 1780), founded pleasure gardens in Scarborough, and his son, again a William (1817-1864), was a botanist whose collections are preserved in the City of Liverpool Museum and the Yorkshire Museum. William Bean himself (1787-1866) was a famous geologist and conchologist; he may have been related to William Jackson Bean (1863-1947) formerly Curator of the Royal Botanic Gardens, Kew, and may have been related by marriage to the geologist William Smith.

Bean's main collections were sold in 1859, the British Museum bought half the collection, for £300, and the Y.P.S. bought one-third for the sum of £200. The final one-sixth was taken by two private collectors one of whom was the Scarborough geologist John Leckenby. The Leckenby collection is now in the Sedgwick Museum, but detective work among labels on material in the Yorkshire Museum collections shows that some of the Bean material was passed from Leckenby to William Reed and hence joined that already in the Yorkshire Museum.

The unique specimens were divided proportionately between the purchasers, the division being made by Dallas and Woodward of the B.M. It was arranged that the British Museum should have all those published by Morris and Lycett, while the Y.P.S. should take those figured by John Phillips, and by Young and Bird, both authors of works on the Geology of Yorkshire. The total number of specimens obtained for the Yorkshire Museum was around 5,000 and included not only many local fossils but also material from other localities in Britain and Europe which assisted in filling up gaps in the general collection. The addition of Bean's material to the Yorkshire fossils already in the Society's possession led the Council to state 'that there will be no finer local Geological collection to be seen anywhere'.

The new rooms were opened to the public during 1859, and Dallas continued to rearrange the geological collections; one feature of the new displays was that he sorted out as many of Phillips' figured fossils as he

Pl. 8. *View from the Yorkshire Fossil Room into the Saurian Gallery, late 19th century. The large ichthyosaur on the left hand wall behind the glass doors remains a major feature of the Museum's displays*

could find among the Bean collection and the Y.P.S. material and marked them with green labels.

By the end of 1860 the pressure of work, perhaps complicated by personal difficulties, were apparently affecting Dallas, and Council requested that work on the Yorkshire Collection should be speeded up; in early 1861 he was asked to move the Kirkdale Cave bones into the Yorkshire Geological Room. This completed, the geological collections were in order, with a fine series of local geology in one room, and a general collection, in the original Geology Gallery, of some 8,000 specimens covering much of the British Isles, with some continental material for comparison.

One eminent name associated with the collections at this period is that of John Frederick Blake (1839-1906). Blake was born in Surrey and educated at Christ's Hospital, London, and Caius College, Cambridge, where he excelled in mathematics, and studied geology under Sedgwick. He was ordained in 1862, and became a curate for three years until 1865, when he took up the post of Mathematical Master and Assistant Chaplain at St. Peter's School in York.

Blake played an active role in the Y.P.S., and from 1870 onwards produced a stream of valuable geological papers; the first five of which were published while he was still at York and dealt with Yorkshire subjects. He left York in 1876 for London and then Nottingham, where he was Professor of Natural Sciences; he was also actively involved with the Geological Society, the Geologists' Association and the International Geological Congress.

By 1863 there were complaints about Dallas' repeated absences from the Museum, and general neglect of the interests of the Society, which he answered with a frank letter admitting the truth of the charges, explaining that 'for some months past I have been in an unsettled and anxious state of mind', but he had now been relieved from the chief cause of his anxieties and hoped to make up for lost time, at which:

'The Committee hopes that since Mr. Dallas now fairly understands the nature of his duties, and since he had expressed his regret for his past omissions he may henceforth by zealously promoting the interests of the Society obtain the confidence of the Members and justify the Council in retaining him as Keeper of the Museum.'

The editorial and translating duties which Dallas had taken on in connection with the *Zoological Record* and other journals must however have continued to take up more of his time than was acceptable to certain members of the Society, and by November 1866 there were again complaints 'in respect of the discharge of the duties as Keeper of the Museum' and in particular that he had neglected the geological collections.

These were answered by an aggrieved letter from Dallas to the effect that the summer Exhibition in York, which had been attended by the Prince and Princess of Wales, had brought so many excursionists to the Museum that apart from the extra attention which they required, 'while they were in the Museum their noise and bustle rendered work quite impossible'. As Council were not satisfied with this answer, noting that they had 'reason to believe that he does not occupy himself with the affairs of the Society during the whole time he is required to remain in the Museum'. Dallas wrote a further letter in which he explained that:

'as all my work had reference to scientific matters and nearly the whole of it is of that description which combines great labor in its execution with very inadequate remuneration I might be regarded as to a certain extent, indirectly, fulfilling the duties of my office. In the case of the *Zoological Record* which for the last two years had occupied the chief part of my own time, this seemed to be still more strongly the case, as the object of this work is most directly the advancement of scientific Zoology . . .'

No discussion of the matter is recorded, and it was not until April 1868 that Rudston Read returned to the attack, complaining about Dallas' dereliction of duty:

'I understand the Office of Curator to the Museum is to take care of the whole collection, and the portion requiring especial and constant attention is the birds and insects, as the minerals will take care of themselves.'

Dallas was able to reply to this in detail, listing all the treatments which he and Graham had tried over the past four years against the moths in the bird collection; that the treatments had proved to a certain extent ineffective was not through lack of care and concern. Some of the specimens were by then 40 years old and their conservation presented difficulties for which remedies were not then available.

In addition, many of the galleries were overcrowded, with specimens on shelves from floor to ceiling. At the A.G.M. in February 1869 a new member, Mr. E. Allen, complained that in order to see all the geological specimens 'a gentleman had on one occasion got upon the back of a friend'.

Dallas' Resignation

It was presumably without much regret that Dallas offered his resignation to the Y.P.S. in November 1868, when he was elected to the post of Assistant Secretary to the Geological Society, to which he was recommended by Professor Huxley as 'one of the hardest workers that I know'. He held this post for 21 years until his death at the age of 67, and during this period edited the *Annals and Magazine of Natural History* and, for a while, *Popular Science Review*. Strangely on his death the Geological Society in their Proceedings gave him no more than a paragraph's mention, and it was left to the Geological Magazine to publish a full obituary.

It was now resolved by Council that the appointment of a Keeper be suspended for six months and that Charles Wakefield, who by now was Drawing Master at Elmfield College, be asked to take charge of the Museum on the same terms as on the last occasion. In March 1869 Percy Ullathorne was appointed to the post of temporary Keeper until the end of the year at a salary of £80 – he was to take instructions from the Honorary Curators. He resigned three months later due to ill-health, and Mr. Wakefield was again called in.

A sub-committee was appointed to define more closely the duties of the Keeper and his relationship with the Honorary Curators; the main points of its report were that the Keeper should devote all his time while at the Museum to the affairs of the Society; that if the post of Assistant Secretary was still to be united with that of Keeper its duties should be more accurately defined; that the Keeper should take charge of all collections and keep all registers, etc.; and that he should give assistance to the Honorary Curators when required.

Appointment of Charles Wakefield

Mr. Wakefield was now appointed to the post of Keeper, with Tuesday and Friday afternoons off to take his classes at the College. Rudston Read was still concerned and, complaining about the inaccessibility of the Allis collection wrote, perhaps with some justification, 'Mr. Wakefield was away giving a dancing or drawing lesson and had this precious key in his pocket . . .' (Council Minutes, 5th December 1870).

There were further complaints at the Annual General Meeting on 7th February 1871 when Mr. Grayston, having criticised the Society's financial arrangements, and having made 'some remarks depreciatory of a former curator' which were greeted with cries of 'shame', continued 'They have a learned gentleman who confined himself to one of the rooms, and as they could not give him such a sum as would secure the whole of his services to the Society, he was doing something else for his own pecuniary advantage'.

He continued, to applause, to attack the management of the Museum, including Proctor's care of the geological collections. Blake spoke in support of Grayston, but suggested that the problem was not one of finance, but that the Society was run 'rather by the fear of offending people than for the advantage of the Society'. He suggested that 'The Council were afraid that a gentleman who had been of great value to the Society would be a candidate for the office, and they felt they dared not oppose him'.

This criticism was denied by both North and Proctor and after more acrimonious discussion the chairman closed the subject by reminding the members that Vernon Harcourt, now in his eighties, was unable to be present and requesting 'let not his last years be pained by any resolution they might pass'.

Within 18 months Proctor resigned the Honorary Curatorship of the geology department. Council debated the appointment of a Curator at the end of 1872, but nothing was done, save to remind Wakefield that his appointment as Keeper was only temporary, and to note that 'he must not purchase for himself or any other person any specimen or curiosity, whether it be brought to the Museum or not, unless previously rejected on behalf of the Museum by the Secretary or Curator of the department to which it belong'. However, it was to be almost 10 years before a new Keeper was appointed.

John Phillips died in April 1874, after a fall at Oxford; he was 73. His body was brought to York, a procession of some 150 dons accompanying his coffin from the Oxford University Museum to the railway station. At York, it was brought to the Yorkshire Museum and placed in the entrance hall, the interior of which had been draped with black cloth.

The next day, it was carried in funeral procession to St. Olave's Church, next to his old home of St. Mary's Lodge, for the first part of the funeral service. As the Big Peter bell of York Minster tolled, the hearse then moved through the centre of York, followed by over 30 carriages of mourners from York, Oxford and London. Along the route the shops had closed and the blinds were drawn in private houses; several business meetings had been altered as a mark of respect. In the York Cemetery, Phillips' body was placed next to that of his sister, in the spot which they had chosen.

There can be no doubt that the love and respect that Phillips felt for his adopted City were returned in full by its citizens. He had hoped to retire to York, and, whatever his duties elsewhere in the country, had never ceased to take an active interest in the Philosophical Society and Museum. Vernon Harcourt had died in 1871, so with Phillips' death the Museum lost the last of its founders.

However there was now a generation of York citizens who as children had seen the Museum grow from its early beginnings. Three who may have been encouraged, even if only at a distance, by the enthusiasm of Vernon Harcourt and John Phillips were now to make their own contribution to the Museum; they were J. F. Walker, W. H. Hudleston and W. Reed.

John Francis Walker (1839-1907)

John Francis Walker (pl. 9) was born in York son of a Freeman and grandson of a Sheriff of the City, and studied under James Buckman at

Pl. 9.   John Francis Walker. Oil painting, artist and date unknown

the Cirencester Royal Agricultural College, at Sidney Sussex College Cambridge, and at Bonn University. He then studied Law and was called to the Bar, but never practised, returning to Cambridge where he lectured in chemistry for a period. He did not marry until he was 43, and then returned to York, spending most of his time on his geological research, specialising in Jurassic brachiopoda. The Yorkshire geologist G. W. Lamplugh, in the *Geological Magazine's* obituary of Walker, shows that Walker was not only an outstanding taxonomist, but also was ahead of his time in appreciating the broader problems of the discipline.

'Although his collection of the Mesozoic Brachiopoda – his favourite and lifelong study – was probably the most extensive that has ever been made, his saying was always – "We want more material! We must wait until we have sufficient material!". And it was his grasp of the broader problems of his subject that led him to this attitude, and not merely the spirit of the collector. The fundamental principle of his method found expression in his favourite dictum: "It would be good for palaeontology if all type-specimens should be destroyed!" – and most workers who have striven to follow the recent developments of palaeontological science will apprehend the truth that underlies this paradox. Walker, firmly holding the evolutionary idea to which his work had led him, recognised that "the true type of a species is its centre, where the individuals are most thickly clustered and most closely resemble each other" and that "a named figured specimen is only a fixed point" which may, or may not, happen to be near or within the central cluster of the species. Hence, he said, no single individual can adequately represent a species, and the so-called species based on type-specimens are of unequal value and often misleading.'

His type specimens he presented to the British Museum and to the Geological Society's Museum, and his generosity in obtaining material for other workers, and in presenting series of specimens was exceptional.

He first started collecting material for the Yorkshire Museum when at Cirencester, and 'kindly promised to lose no opportunity of obtaining fossils from the strata of that locality.' Although his major contributions to the Museum occur later, from 1880 onwards, it seems probable that, even as a young man, on his visits to his family in York he would have kept in touch with the geologically minded members of the Y.P.S., to their mutual benefit.

Wilfrid Hudleston (1828-1909)

Wilfrid Hudleston was born in York as Wilfrid Simpson; his mother being heiress to the Hudlestons of Cumberland, he took their name in 1867. Educated at St. Peter's School York and St. John's College Cambridge he spent some time studying Law and was called to the Bar, but never practised. This was followed by a considerable amount of foreign travel, his main interest at that time being ornithology. He then studied natural history and chemistry at Edinburgh and at the Royal College of Chemistry in London. He was introduced to Professor John Morris who enlisted him into the ranks of the geologists, in which he ultimately obtained the distinction of being elected President of the Geologists' Association in 1881, and President of the Geological Society in 1892. He owned lands in Yorkshire, Northumberland and Dorset, and resided in London for most of his life. In addition to his involvement with the Yorkshire Philosophical Society he was President of the Yorkshire Naturalists' Union. He was also an active Vice-President of the Dorset Natural History and Antiquarian Field Club, and assisted with the geological collections of the Dorset County Museum.

Hudleston was, apart from John Phillips, the most eminent geologist ever connected with the Yorkshire Museum. He held the position of Honorary Keeper of Mineralogy from 1876 until his death over 30 years later, and although, owing to his many commitments and travels he cannot have spent very much time in York, he figured many of the Society's specimens in his monographs on the fossils of the Yorkshire Oolites, and of the Inferior Oolite, and assisted in the re-arrangement of the Jurassic fossil displays. During this period first William Reed, then J. F. Walker held the post of Honorary Keeper of Geology so that the department was not lacking in on-the-spot curatorial care.

William Reed (1810-1892)

However it was William Reed (pl. 10) who made the greatest single geological contribution to the Museum, matching in size and importance the total palaeontological collections formed under the stewardship of Phillips and Charlesworth.

After studying medicine as a pupil of Mr. Ness, of Helmsley, Reed went to St. George's Hospital, London and, after a period in Paris, to the Royal College of Surgeons. For a while he was resident medical officer at the York County Hospital, then moved into private practice in and around York, where he remained for the rest of his life. He was able to devote his later years and, it seems, a considerable amount of money to building up his geological collection.

On his death the *Yorkshire Herald* said:

'Mr. Reed was of a retiring disposition, and took little interest in public affairs. He was, however, of a genial disposition, and in private life was a pleasant companion. He never married and lived an extremely abstemious life, performing many acts of private charity and benevolence which the world saw not . . .'

93

Pl. 10.   William Reed. Oil painting, artist and date unknown

There seems to be no record of any formal education in geology, nor of the influences leading Reed along this path. However by the end of his life he had built up a very comprehensive library of geological works (which he donated to the Museum), and it is not unreasonable to assume that the facilities at the Museum, and the presence of John Phillips, William Vernon Harcourt, Edward Charlesworth and William Dallas, as well as many other geological members of the Y.P.S. may have been his main influence. Reed became Honorary Curator of Geology in 1873, a post which he held till his death in 1892, and was elected to Council in 1874.

In August 1878 he wrote to the Y.P.S.:

'Being the possessor of an extensive series of fossils derived from the different beds and strata of which the British Isles are composed extending from the Pleistocene of Post-Tertiary to the Cambrian illustrating the variety of life that existed at the different periods of time also a series of recent osteological specimens and recent British shells valuable to compare with extinct and more ancient forms, as the collection contains not only numerous species but even whole series that are either absent or inadequately represented in the Museum of the Yorkshire Philosophical Society, it would give me great pleasure under certain conditions and restrictions to present the whole to the Society to be amalgamated with the Museum collection viz. that sufficient space should be provided by the Council for its reception – the Tertiary series and other delicate and fragile shells to be kept in the glass boxes and not removed and fixed upon tablets by any adhesive matter which would materially detract from their value – that a mark distinguishing them from the specimens belonging at present to the Museum be attached – the Stratigraphical arrangement to be strictly adhered to – the smaller examples are placed in cabinets containing 291 drawers the larger in upright cases.

'I feel anxious to see my collections incorporated with those in the Museum as soon as possible and I shall be happy to assist in doing so but as my health is not good [Reed suffered from bronchitis] I must ask the Council to provide someone who can work under my instructions. In conclusion let me express my earnest wishes for the future prosperity of the Museum and to assure you how happy I feel to be able to do something for the principal institution in the City in which I have spent the greater part of my professional life.'

This collection, which was acknowledged in detail in the Annual Report of the Society, proved to consist of some 42,000 specimens.

'The collection presented by Mr. Reed has been formed at great cost over a period of many years, and has been well known to geologists as one of the most valuable private collections in the United Kingdom. The Council congratulate the Society on its acquisition of a collection, which, when displayed in the Society's rooms, will raise our Museum to the first rank among similar scientific Institutions in this country.'

Letters and catalogues preserved with the collection show that Edward Charlesworth was obtaining important material for Reed during the period of 1871-1878, especially the Whincopp and the Baker collections of Crag fossils (Pyrah, 1979). The style of the letters, and a reference to previous catalogues – alas not preserved – show that Charlesworth had been in correspondence with Reed for some time previously. His obituary in the *Geological Magazine* (1893) confirms this:

'On Mr. Charlesworth's retirement from York, in 1858, he settled for a time in London, and carried on a Natural History and Geological Agency . . . Encouraged and supported by Mr. William Reed, of York, Edward Charlesworth was, for many years, one of the most active buyers of fossils in London; always seeking to secure the best specimens and paying the highest prices for them. In fact he devoted himself almost solely to the purchase of specimens for Mr. Reed and the British Museum . . .'

While the Geological Society obituary states that although Charlesworth supplied specimens to the British Museum 'he generally had some exquisite specimen, temptingly displayed on pink cotton wool in a glass-topped box, for his private customers, of whom Mr. Reed, of York must always be deemed the chief', the story of the Whincopp collection shows that Charlesworth was quite willing to bid against the British Museum on Reed's behalf.

William Whincopp (1795-1874) was a wine merchant and collector of geological and antiquarian objects from the neighbourhood of his home town of Woodbridge, Suffolk. By 1871 he was in considerable debt to his bank and instituted proceedings for bankruptcy; a transcript of the proceedings is held by the Suffolk Record Office. Whincopp's main aim was to keep his collection intact; he tried to explain that he had formed it not for the purpose of collection but 'to illustrate and explain matters which have created a great sensation of late – that is to say many have supposed that man is much older than the Mosaic account represents him to be . . .'

Whincopp had made some half-hearted efforts to sell his collection to relieve his financial difficulties; the British Museum had made him one offer which he had turned down as being inadequate. He then passed the collection to his Bankers, Messrs. Alexander, before going to the Bankruptcy Court, thus removing it from the reach of his creditors, hoping, unrealistically, to be able to redeem it later. Charlesworth wrote to Reed:

'113a Strand. Octor. 24-71

Dear Reed,

'During my late Suffolk excursion I devoted one whole morning to a careful examination of the Whincopp Collection now at the Woodbridge Bank where it is held as security for an overdrawn account.

'During my occasional calls upon Mr. Whincopp between the years 1840 and 1860 I could never get him to let me see the whole collection. In fact he seemed to take a pride in tantalising his Geological visitors . . . But as the Collection is now in the Market, the present possessors naturally wish to show the whole of it . . . I found the collection surpass my expectations . . . a multitude of beautiful things of the highest interest – many of them unique.

'. . . I at once wrote to the Bank offering provisionally to take the Collection at an advance of £75 above the Brit. Museum . . . Now in the event of my offer being taken, I should be able to offer the Collection and prepare a copious Catalogue for £250 . . .'

Charlesworth evidently did not have the wherewithal to purchase the collection himself for subsequent resale, so had to persuade Reed to lend him the money. On 30th October he wrote:

'I am greatly puzzled to comprehend why the fact of the Collection being for sale should have been kept apparently so quiet. I can't hear that Mr. Whincopp has told any of his numerous geological acquaintances; and the Messrs. Alexander appear to have told only the British Museum people, and the British Museum passed the news on to me . . .

'I went up this morning to the British Museum and I asked Mr. Waterhouse and Mr. Woodward frankly to say whether or not the British Museum authorities were disposed to make any advance on their original offer. I found Mr. Waterhouse not disposed to be communicative, but Mr. Woodward told me that the question of an advance in the British Museum offer, would depend upon the share which the Jermyn St. Museum would be willing to take . . .

'Now if you see your way *financially* to put it in my power to offer such terms to Mr. Alexanders that they may call to mind the old proverb "a bird in the hand is worth two in the bush" and supposing that no *third* party steps in, I think our chance of securing the collection would be very good . . .

'Now supposing you were willing to guarantee say £200, and *I* could manage as I dare say I could £30 to £35, then I should be in a position to deal with Messrs. Alexander unconditionally. . . . At Woodbridge Mr. Searles Wood has a nephew a highly respected Solicitor, and I could employ him to draw up a short deed assigning the Collection, Cabinets and Proceeds of Duplicates to you for the advance or the guarantee of £200 and to the Revd. D. I. Heath from whom I would expect to have the loan of the £35.

'Then I could pack and remove the entire collection with Cabinets here 113a Strand, of which establishment Mr. Henson is the Tennant under the Crown . . . Then I should lose no time in pricing, cataloguing and getting off to you some of the finest things, and at the same time looking out a set of Duplicates for Jermyn St. . . . I think there would be a great advantage in giving Davies of the B.M. a sight of the things as I catalogue them . . .'

In view of the financial difficulties which Charlesworth had had with the Y.P.S. some 20 years earlier it is interesting to find that on 5th November 1871 he wrote:

97

'. . . and if the money passes in any way thro' a York bank, I should prefer my name not being introduced for reasons which I can explain at a future time . . .'

Charlesworth catalogued and sent off the material to Reed in batches during 1872 and 1873, as his health allowed:

'Jan. 9th 1872. Dear Reed, I am supplementing my favourite beverages of Tea and Coffee with an ample quantity of Port-wine and Stout, and I find I am making good progress on the road to recovery, but I am not strong enough yet to renew my visits to the British Museum, College of Surgeons &c in connection with the identification and comparison of the Whincopp fossils . . .'

Charlesworth's catalogues list some 450 specimens, the cream of the collection, which came to York to supplement Reed's already fine Crag collections, including specimens figured by Ray Lankester.

The 41 letters and voluminous catalogues demonstrate the extent of Charlesworth's influence on Reed's collection and suggests a certain dependence on Reed's financial support. It is obvious that Charlesworth was well informed as to the extent of the collection, knew its strengths and weaknesses, and actively sought out material that might be available for sale, in order to improve it. Before passing specimens on to Reed he obtained expert advice, where necessary, as to its identification and comparison with material in other collections. He then sent catalogues to Reed, so that the latter could indicate his requirements. Reed rarely decided against the purchase of items on the list.

There seems no evidence that Charlesworth's interest in fossil dealing was primarily a pecuniary one, or that his main interest was in Reed's money. Indeed all biographical details show that Charlesworth was above all a collector and curator, and there can be little doubt that his prime motives in his dealings with Reed were those of concern for the specimens and the collection. Perhaps it is not too far-fetched to suggest that, having little money of his own and finding that the position of employee did not suit his temperament, this was his way of building up a collection which he could think of, to a certain extent, as his own contribution to science. His friendship with Reed can be seen as one of complementary personalities; opposite in character, yet they shared not only the same fascination with fossils but also the same attitude to curation; like Charlesworth, William Reed would spend hours copying out information in his small neat handwriting onto the specimen labels and carefully arranging the fragile specimens in their glass-topped boxes. Charlesworth knew that specimens which he sold to Reed would be looked after as well as if they were in his own collection. His hopes for the ultimate fate of this collection are revealed in a letter to Phillips:

'The gift of your charming and valuable book is at this time especially welcome . . . I have secured the famous Whincopp Crag Collection. Mr. Reed of York is to add to the Treasures of his already Magnificent collection of the fossils of the Crag by a selection from the Whincopp cabinets. When he has received this, the Reed Museum at York so far as Crag fossils are concerned will throw into the shade every other collection in the Kingdom . . . It is very unlikely that another such collection of the Crag fossils will or indeed can ever be made; and I sometimes indulge a hope that my Friend Reed may bequeath his Palaeontological wealth to the Museum of that City in which professionally he holds so honourable a position.'

(O.U.M. 1871.81/2)

William Whincopp died in 1874 and a second collection of fossils was sold at auction and purchased by Charlesworth, who offered them to Reed, as before. In his introduction to the catalogue Charlesworth mentions that the collection includes:

'one or two rarities which if good faith had been kept with the Woodbridge Bank ought to have been transferred to Alexander and Co. when the first collection was made to them . . .'

In October 1875 Charlesworth sent to Reed the first of a series of catalogues of Red Crag material collected by another Woodbridge resident, Mr. Baker, a local watchmaker, which also included much rare material, as well as further specimens figured by Lankester.

The last catalogue is dated 6th December 1878, and may represent the end of Charlesworth's more vigorous activities as a dealer, for his obituary in the *Quarterly Journal of the Geological Society* for 1894 states:

'The last 20 years of his life were greatly clouded by long and severe illness, frequently confining him to his bedroom, and almost entirely preventing him from doing anything in the way of searching for fossils.'

Much of Reed's collection of some 42,000 choice specimens must have come, through Charlesworth and other dealers, from previous collections, and research workers who have seen the material suggest that it may contain portions of important early 19th century collections which were disposed of in the 1850's and 1860's and have since been presumed 'lost'.

During 1875 members of the Geologists' Association visited the Yorkshire Museum and then went to see Reed's 'splendid geological collection'. After donating it to the Museum in 1878 Reed arranged the specimens in the Museum's galleries, and also worked through the Society's reserve collections, sorting out material of scientific rarity and placing it on display.

Reed continued to enrich the Society's Museum each year with valuable material, and in 1880 he purchased for the Y.P.S. the collection of the late Edward Wood, of Richmond, Yorkshire. Wood was the wealthy President of the Richmond and North Riding Club, who frequently paid all the expenses of the club's field trips, such as chartering a special train for an excursion to Scarborough (Allen, 1976). His superb collection of some 10,000 specimens from the Carboniferous rocks around Richmond included many described and figured by L. G. de Koninck and by T. Davidson.

In 1885 Reed gave the Museum a collection of about 1,000 specimens for teaching purposes; at the A.G.M. on 2nd February 1886 a Mr. Gough pointed out that 'the specimens etc. were noted all over Europe for their excellency, being type specimens, and of the utmost value from a scientific and teaching point of view'. Reed's collection did indeed contain many Type and Figured specimens, and it is possible that he kept them back, together with the cream of the material, until the bulk of his collections had already been safely assimilated into the Museum's care and he could be sure of the safety of the Type material but it may be that Gough was using the term 'type' in a looser sense. In 1887 Reed gave the Y.P.S. a collection of about 2,500 specimens from the Inferior Oolite of Dorset and Somerset, and 500 fossils from the Carboniferous rocks of Yoredale, Leyburn, Wensleydale, which included 43 figured specimens (presumably the Carboniferous fish teeth figured by J. W. Davis 1883, 1884). In 1889 he donated a large collection of fossils from the English Tertiary and Irish Carboniferous Limestone which are recorded as being collected by Charlesworth. In 1891 he again donated several hundred fossils from localities ranging from Scotland to Cornwall, and on his death in 1892 bequeathed collections of Aust Cliff Rhaetic material (which has since proved to contain 'lost' figured insect specimens), of Scottish Carboniferous Polyzoa, Australian Tertiary fossils and Pleistocene molluscs, as well as the Elwes collection of Hampshire Tertiary fossils, an important acquisition which came on the market in late 1891 (Torrens, Getty and Crane, 1978); the locality suggests that Charlesworth, with his Hampshire contacts, may have been instrumental in obtaining it.

William Reed spent much of his time in the Museum, and in October 1883 Mr. Noble reported to the monthly meeting the:

'very valuable services of the Curator of Geology . . . Mr. Reed was now carrying on alone that work which the services of the Keeper of the Museum were obtained to perform. Indeed he did not know how the executive could have carried on the business of the Society without the valuable aid of Mr. Reed . . . Every day he was at his post in the geological room, and was always ready to impart information to anyone who asked respecting his department.'

As well as his collections Reed bequeathed to the Museum his extensive library of geological and zoological works, to be known as the Reed Reference Library, and the sum of £600, the interest to be used to purchase further books.

100

William Reed gave to the Yorkshire Museum at least 60,000 specimens, at a conservative estimate – the true total may have been much higher. The collection requires much more specialist research before its importance can be fully evaluated, containing as it does comprehensive series of choice fossils from almost all the classic 19th century palaeontological sites, and much Type material.

The Society and the Theory of Evolution

What we now see as one of the major scientific controversies of the 19th century, Darwin's Theory of Evolution, seems to have had little immediate impact on the work of the Society. Its slow acceptance can be traced in the reports of lectures given by Society members and the subsequent discussions and correspondence, as reported in the York papers. We can only guess at the animated discussions which must have taken place between the more conservative of the Society's officers and the more progressive, such as their Keeper Dallas, who counted Darwin among his friends.

Although *The Origin of Species* was published in 1859, there does not seem to be any reference to Darwin's work in Y.P.S. reports until March 1862, in a lecture by S. W. North 'On the relation of Man to the Lower Animals'. At the conclusion of his talk 'the lecturer at some length endeavoured to show how the fallacy of the various theories of development which have from time to time been advocated, and the absence of support from zoological evidence . . . led inevitably to the conclusion that species are immutable'.

Eighteen months later in November 1863, North returned to the subject and lectured to the Society 'On the various theories which have been advanced to explain the origin of species'. In this he discussed the theories of Agassiz, Owen, Larmarck and Darwin, but regretted that 'time would not allow him to enter into the arguments by which it was sought to refute the various theories'. The question of evolution was 'a scientific investigation [which] demanded attentive consideration [but was] not yet removed beyond the bounds of hypothesis'.

The Reverend T. Myers, offering the vote of thanks, commented that the lecture had been 'a very able lecture of a kind in perfect harmony with the spirit of a philosophical institution' and the vote was carried unanimously. However, at least one member of the audience felt he had to express opposition to Darwin's ideas, as the correspondence column of the

101

Yorkshire Gazette also carried a letter from 'J.T.' 'One of our northern lights has been attempting by flickering corruscations to illumine our city . . . on the subject of "The Origin of Species" . . . what are the phantasmogoric objects conjured up by the Aurora from the fertile fancies of the Lamarcks, the Darwins, *et hoc genus omni*, but a monstrous nightmare brood . . . ?'

In 1866 Darwin's champion Thomas Huxley was elected an Honorary Member, and early the next year Dallas gave a lecture on 'The Darwinian Hypothesis' in which he detailed the results of entomological investigations by Bates, Wallace and Wollaston 'which seem to tend in favour of the hypothesis of evolution from pre-existing forms, although many more such laborious investigations will be necessary before it can take its place as a theory . . .' At the next A.G.M., in 1868, Darwin was elected an Honorary Member, and the Society purchased for its library a copy of *The Origin of Species* – nearly 10 years after its publication.

This did not necessarily mean that Darwin's theory was generally accepted within the Society. At a meeting in November 1868 Proctor, the Honorary Curator of Geology, lecturing on Pterodactyles, stated that he 'could not see that there was any more evidence for the development of the lower into the higher forms of animals than that there were special laws of creation for each animal', and in 1872, after a lecture by F. Needham on the relationship of the Negro to the rest of the human race, North, in his vote of thanks, said that although Darwin had 'collected a large number of facts, and worked his theory out in a clever style, it was by no means proved up to the present time'.

The question was then more or less ignored for a decade, until the appointment of Henry Plantnauer to the post of Keeper at the end of 1883. In April 1884 he lectured to the Society on the subject of trilobites, and although not denying Darwin's theory entirely, he criticised it in detail, suggesting that it needed modifying.

The subject was taken up by the Society's conchologists, and later that year the Reverend W. C. Hey read a paper on snail shells, after which Dr. Matterson, from the Chair, 'thought that Mr. Hey had proved in a very philosophical sort of way that there was a sort of evolution even in these lower animals'. He went on to say that 'However much there may be said against it, there really was nothing objectionable to the theory of evolution, as many people imagined, because it did not at all throw aside the idea of creation'. Evidently members of the Society were coming to terms with Darwin's theory according to their individual consciences, once they realised it was here to stay.

102

Eighteen months later, in December 1885, Platnauer gave a lecture on 'The Evolution of the Limb' after which North moved that Platnauer had 'proved the truth of the doctrine of evolution, which rested upon a solid basis'. North was by then an elder statesman of the Society, and his acceptance of Darwin's theory, after 25 years of philosophical questioning, marked the end of controversy within the Society on this topic.

The Society effectively distanced itself from scientific controversy, but in doing so also moved away from the stimulating influence of scientific discovery, so that during the 20th century its scientific role became largely that of maintaining the collections and using them for educational purposes.

CHAPTER 7

Into the 20th Century (1878-1940)

John-Clay Purves (18251903)

In 1878 Mr. Wakefield was given notice from his post as temporary Keeper. From several capable applicants the person chosen was Dr. J.-C. Purves, who was offered a temporary job helping William Reed; this was made a permanent post after the death of Henry Baines the next year. John-Clay Purves was a Scot with relatives in Belgium. He qualified in Medicine at Edinburgh University, and as an army doctor travelled widely before becoming attached to the Geological Survey in Edinburgh for a couple of years. Details of his career are given in the Belgian *Biographie Nationale*, but as he stayed at the Yorkshire Museum for barely two years only a few salient points will be mentioned here.

Purves' qualifications for the post are obscure. His biographer could find no mention of his name in the records of the Geological Survey, nor did he publish the research he did while travelling the world. Purves was a nervous, sensitive and temperamental man, dogged by ill-health and bad luck, and his subsequent career in the Belgian Geological Survey was erratic, but his geological work, in particular on the Namurian, which he named, was sound and during this later period, from his 55th year to his 73rd year, he made a lasting contribution to the knowledge of Belgian geology. However, it is unlikely that such a person would have settled into the curatorial world, and in June 1880 Purves – who was on holiday at the time – wrote advising the Council of his appointment to the Belgian Geological Survey, and resigning from the end of August.

Walter Keeping (1854-1888)

By August 1880 the Council were unanimous in offering the post to Walter Keeping, the son of the Curator of the Sedgwick Museum. Walter Keeping's early career in geology had been brilliant; pursuing a scholarship at Christ College Cambridge while working with his father Henry Keeping

104

in the Museum, he studied the Neocomian of the Cambridge area, and was to be awarded the Sedgwick prize in 1883 for this work. He left the Sedgwick Museum to take up the Chair of Natural Science in the University College of Wales at Aberystwith, and turned his attention to the geology of that area. In addition to these major publications he had also published various notes and observations on palaeontological and geological discoveries made by him in Britain and on the Continent.

Tragically this early promise of a distinguished career was not to be fulfilled, as soon after taking up the appointment at York he developed the first symptoms of the illness from which he was to die a few years later, at the age of 34. The seriousness of his illness, a form of paralysis, was not fully realised at first, and the Council minutes record dissatisfaction with his work and his attitude towards the Curators, and lengthy periods of illness. He resigned in 1883 'as a result of mental infirmity', after intercession by his father the Council awarded him half a year's salary.

Fortunately for the Society, as we have already seen William Reed stepped into the breach during this period and carried out many of the Keeper's day to day duties, as well as organising the transfer of his own and other collections to the geology department of the Museum.

Henry Maurice Platnauer (1857-1939)

The next appointment to the post of Keeper was that of Henry Maurice Platnauer (pl. 11), and the Society found that it was a case of 'third time lucky'. Platnauer, educated at the City of London School and London University, had spent eight years on the staff of the British Museum (Natural History) in the mineralogy department. As his letter of acceptance of the Yorkshire Museum post was written from the B.M. (N.H.) it seems that the *Museums Journal* obituary may be mistaken in suggesting that he was already in York, where his wife's invalid father lived.

Platnauer was a keen part-time soldier throughout his life, later serving in training units in the 1914-1918 war, with the rank of Captain. This suggests the possession of a certain degree of robustness and practicality which must have aided him in dealing with the various, often opposing, requirements and personalities of the Honorary Curators and Council members more successfully than had previous Keepers. Indeed Platnauer was, apart from John Phillips, the only Keeper to fully gain the respect of the Society, and to be nominated Vice-President, after his resignation from the Keepership in 1904.

The main task that faced Platnauer, in the geological department, was the assimilation of the 50-60,000 specimens given by William Reed during the 1880's. Much of the work was no doubt done by Reed himself, when his

Pl. 11.   Henry Maurice Platnauer. Keeper of the Museum and joint founder, in 1889, of the Museums' Association

failing health permitted, with assistance from J. F. Walker and other members of the Society. The dedication of Platnauer's approach is shown by the fact that by the time most of this material had come into the Museum – and before Reed's death – he had prepared for publication in the Society's Proceedings (1891) a Catalogue of Type and figured material in the Reed collections and the other collections previously in the possession of the Society. An appendix published in 1894 lists mainly specimens figured since 1890. Together some 390 specimens are recorded. Unfortunately this catalogue, published only in the Society's Proceedings never became widely distributed and soon slipped into obscurity.

With various restrictions, Council allowed Platnauer to undertake geological excursions to study the Yorkshire rocks 'when directed to do so by Mr. Reed', and, in January 1887, although expressing disapproval, allowed him to lecture at The Mount School (a Quaker girls' school) once a week for six months. In October 1900 he was given permission to make up a loan collection of fossils and minerals to be lent to local schools. Whether or not his school lectures continued is not recorded.

After the death of William Reed in May 1892 J. F. Walker was elected as Honorary Curator in Geology, in March 1893. Walker sorted out duplicates from the Reed collection and from their sale raised £30, with which he purchased glass-topped boxes for the more fragile specimens in the Reed collection.

Over the years from 1867 Walker had donated several thousand geological specimens to the Museum; his own collection, which filled six cases, came to the Museum on his death in 1907.

With E. Howarth of Sheffield City Museum, Platnauer was responsible for the formation of the Museums' Association in 1889. Although his obituary in the *Museums Journal* states that he was acting 'on behalf of the Yorkshire Philosophical Society' the Society's Council Minutes for February 1888 record that Platnauer was given permission to write to other Curators with a view to forming 'an association of Museums for mutual help'. It seems probable that it was Platnauer who first broached the subject to Council, possibly with the aims of improving the status of the post of salaried Museum Keeper, as well as strengthening the position of museums in the country. With Howarth he remained Joint Secretary and Editor of the Annual Report of the Museums' Association until 1896. In 1911 he was elected President of the Association.

Viewed from a distance, the turn of the century can be seen as marking the turn of fortunes of the geology department of the Museum, as after 70 years of being one of the main growth areas of the Museum, it moved into a care and maintenance phase. While this could perhaps be correlated to a certain extent with the change of public fashion away from geology to natural history and archaeology, the Yorkshire Museum never had been a 'Museum of Curiosities' formed to attract the public; the basic purpose of the Museum was to safeguard material of importance to systematic taxonomists, and research interest in the collections continued as before.

The position of this one department should rather be seen against a background of the Museum's own struggle for survival within the local economic climate, compounded by the problems created within the Museum by its own success.

From the very beginning the Society, like many similar institutions, had financial problems. York itself was becoming something of an economic backwater; it had lost its position as a sea-port and trading town and missed out on the industrial revolution. George Hudson was 'to make all the railways come to York' but they were not followed by the hoped-for industrial expansion, although the railway and its carriage-works became a major source of employment in the City. While York, during the 19th and early 20th centuries, settled down into the role of an agricultural market town, it did have the advantages of remaining a pleasant place to live, with good rail access to elsewhere in England and Scotland, and therefore retained a core of wealth, invested in land and in the mines and mills of the West Riding.

In order to bridge the gap between subscription income and necessary expenditure the Y.P.S. was able to derive a considerable secondary income (estimated to be around £500 a year in the late 1880's), from admission to the gardens and swimming pool and hire of the marquee.

The Society also tailored the range of lectures offered to attract a wider audience during the second half of the 19th century. Up until the 1850's the lectures were entirely scentific in nature, but in the 1860's both travelogues and literary themes made an appearance, and by the 1890's musical evenings were organised for the members. From 1897 the York and District Field Naturalists took over the provision of geological and natural history lectures in the Museum, and the Society's own programme concentrated on a mixture of general scientific and sociological lectures and travelogues. Thus in 1888 the suffragette Mrs. Fawcett lectured on 'The Social Progress of Women during the last 100 years'.

While the income was, with economies, sufficient to maintain the Museum, it clearly did not allow for expansion, so that as the collections grew drawers had to be fitted into odd spaces, and specimens were hung from walls and balconies (pl. 12). Although Council did occasionally give the Keeper and Honorary Curators the power to dispose of duplicate

Pl. 12.   *The skeleton of the Irish Elk dominates the crowded Bird Room in this late 19th or early 20th century photograph*

material 'by gift, exchange, sale or loan' fortunately for the integrity of the collections this policy was not pursued to any great extent.

The ready availability of local biological and archaeological material led to a tradition of active involvement in these subjects in the local schools, and to a supply of capable young volunteers willing to assist with these subjects in the Museum. In contrast, there was little in York and the surrounding district to encourage the study of geology, except the collections of the Museum itself, and the geology department probably owed its continued existence as a major department of the Museum throughout the 19th century almost entirely to the Society's policy of employing a Keeper whose main interests and qualifications were geological, hence ensuring that material from a wider area was drawn into the Museum, continually strengthening the collections. It was therefore a major blow to the future of the geology department when, with Platnauer's resignation in 1904, this policy was abandoned.

Oxley Grabham

A letter to the new Keeper, Oxley Grabham, a local gentleman with keen sporting interests, 'At this salary we could not expect your full time and should be prepared to accept four days a week allowing the remainder for sport . . .' contrasts with the many admonitions to previous Keepers to devote more time to the Museum, and suggests that financial considerations may have played a major part, the Council evidently accepting that they could not afford to attract a professional curator to the post. That the Society was (as usual) in financial difficulty is further shown by a letter sent the next year to 'Mr. Carnegie, the Millionaire' asking him for a donation towards the cost of arrangements for the reception of the British Association meeting to be held in York in 1906.

Grabham's main interests were natural history, particularly of a sporting nature, and the antiquarian departments, which by then were beginning to be split up into Roman Archaeology, Medieval Archaeology, Numismatics, etc., rather on the basis, one suspects, of the availability of interested Honorary Curators. There seems to be no record of Grabham showing any interest in the geology collections.

At this time another member and benefactor of the Society was gaining fame as a geologist, although in a field far removed from palaeontology.

Tempest Anderson (1846-1913)

Dr. Tempest Anderson (pl. 13) was York born, and studied medicine at University College, London. He then returned to York to follow in his

Pl. 13.   Tempest Anderson (centre) and companions on the rim of the volcano Soufrière in 1907

111

father's medical practice, specialising in ophthalmic medicine. He served the City of York in many ways, and with a practical interest in many aspects of public health – water supply, open spaces, traffic management – he was one of the pioneers of town planning in York, and became Sheriff of the City in 1894. A wealthy practice with two hard-working partners enabled him to indulge in his other interests, photography and science, and to travel widely in their pursuit. A keen mountaineer, at first he seems to have been interested in glaciers, but soon turned to volcanoes, on which he became an acknowledged authority. By 1900 he had visited and photographed most of the classic European volcanoes, as well as those of Iceland, and had travelled across North America. In 1902 the Royal Society asked him to accompany Dr. Flett of the Geological Survey, to study the recent eruptions of Mont Pelée and La Soufrière, in the West Indies. The results of this expedition were probably Anderson's most important contribution to the science, and in the subsequent paper published by the Royal Society he was able to explain the hitherto unknown mechanism of the *nuée ardent* blast, drawing on his experience of similar damage caused by glacial avalanches.

Anderson was much in demand as a lecturer throughout Britain, and became a Council Member of the Royal Geographical, Geological and Linnean Societies, and a Vice-President of the British Association for the Advancement of Science.

In the next few years he visited Southern Africa, Central America, New Zealand and Canada, and Indonesia and the Philippines; he died in the Red Sea on the way home from this last trip.

The immense photographic archive resulting from these travels (some 5,000 negatives), was preserved in the Yorkshire Museum where it still forms a valuable source for volcanological and ethnographic students.

Anderson brought the same dedication and energy (and financial backing) to his involvement with the Philosophical Society, of which he was Secretary and later President, as well as head of the Photographic Section. Over the years he paid for repairs and improvements to the Museum out of his own pocket, and in 1912 added the Tempest Anderson Hall to the Museum buildings, in memory of his sister. This 400-seat lecture theatre freed the old lecture theatre, in the central hall of the Museum, for use as a display gallery, and also improved the basement room below, as the well of the theatre had previously extended down into the basement. In addition a large room was formed under the seating of the new hall; this was fitted up as a storage and reference room for the use of students.

After his death the next year the Society inherited around half of his estate of some £94,000. However, one of the trustees was Oxley Grabham, whose eccentric behaviour in later years, coupled with the casual attitude of Tempest Anderson's solicitor, his cousin Henry Stuart Anderson, meant that the estate was not wound up until 1953. Some of the money was invested in foreign enterprises, which were rendered valueless by the political turmoil of the 1914-1918 war. Nevertheless this bequest considerably eased the financial position of the Society, at least for a while, and the geological department was one of those to benefit.

William Johnson

After J. F. Walker's death in 1907 the Rev. William Johnson (brother of Prof. Thomas Johnson the botanist and palaeobotanist) had taken on responsibility for the palaeontology collections. William Johnson, despite a childhood of relative poverty, had been educated at the Methodist boarding school Elmfield College, in York (where Charles Wakefield was Drawing Master), where he stayed on to become assistant-master, taking a B.A. (London) at that time. By 1885 he was Headmaster of Elmfield, and in 1892 he moved to St. Augustine's Grammar School, Dewsbury, as Headmaster; here he took Holy Orders. In 1897 he returned to York as Headmaster of the ancient school of Archbishop Holgate's.

This school had been founded in 1546 by Robert Holgate, Lord President for the Council for the North and Archbishop of York. By the time of Johnson's appointment, 350 years later, the school 'seemed to many people to be perilously near the end of its long life' (Evans, 1951). Johnson so completely rejuvenated the school, updating the syllabus, building a science block, and encouraging sport, that the number of pupils grew in the 20 years he was there, from 47 to 294, and Johnson was widely regarded as the 'second Founder'. In addition, during this period he also found the time and energy to take a second degree, that of B.Sc. (London).

His interest in geology seems to have been of a general nature; he frequently lectured to the Society on geological topics, and wrote the geology chapter of the local handbook for the 75th meeting of the British Association in York. There is no record of any specific action on the geology collections until shortly before his retirement from Archbishop Holgate's (in 1915) when in January 1914 he appeared before the General Purposes Committee by invitation, and reported that, as he considered geology the most important department of the Museum, a geological Sub-Curator should be appointed. The next month the same committee heard that the fossil collection required remounting and cleaning, although William Watson, the Museum assistant, reported that he had cleaned and dusted all the fossil cases in 1906 for the visit of the British Association, and they had

113

been cleaned again since then. A year later, in January 1915, Johnson successfully proposed in Council that a scheme be considered for relabelling the geological collections. However, Council was busy with other matters, such as warding off suggestions that soldiers and horses should be billeted in the Museum and insuring the Museum against crashing aircraft, and it was not until November that the matter was again discussed, in the General Purposes Committee.

At last, early in 1916, 'a neat-handed girl' Miss Edith Holmes, from the Municipal Secondary School for Girls, was appointed to do the work; Johnson had offered to give two days a week of his time to supervise her. Helped also by William Watson, during the next three years the whole of the geology galleries and cases were cleaned and repainted, and virtually the whole of the geology collection – some 100,000 specimens, were removed from their boards, cleaned, and replaced with new labels, having made 'a comparison of the methods adopted in several institutions . . . in order to arrive at the best paper for remaining clean in appearance, the best ink for durability and the best type for legibility'. Original labels, where present, were preserved on the back of the boards.

By the end of 1916 the Council, expressing their satisfaction at the way the work was being carried out, resolved that the old title of Sub-Curator (which had lapsed on the death of Henry Baines) should be revived for William Watson, who would also receive a donation of five pounds (pl. 14), and that Miss Holmes should have her salary increased from 13/- to 15/- per week. After the geology material was completed she stayed on as general office help, typing, labelling, looking after the library, etc. until her retirement.

Meanwhile the Keeper, Oxley Grabham, was showing symptoms of the nervous illness which was to turn him into an eccentric recluse in later years, and in October 1919 he resigned. He was granted £150 a year for five years, plus a gratuity of £100 for special treatment.

The post of Keeper was advertised in the *Museums Journal*, and the Secretary wrote to the Chief Librarian of the British Museum 'Have you anyone at the British Museum who would be suitable for the post. We should much like another Mr. Platnauer who came to us from you . . .' (22nd March 1920). However no suitable applications were received, and 'it was not considered advisable to appoint a lady to the post' (21st June 1920 – the name of the rejected lady applicant is not recorded).

In January 1921 the post was readvertised, this time in *Nature*; application was limited to those who had received 'a College Education'. From the applicants (who included the geologists, C. N. Bromehead, of the

To

Mr William Watson

We, the Members of the Yorkshire Philosophical Society desire to place on record our high appreciation of the services rendered to the Society by Mr William Watson during a period of Fifty years. During this half century he has served under six Keepers, and rendered special assistance in the Geological department.

His ability as a skilled photographer and lanternist, and his long service and faithful attention to duty merit the highest commendation, and have proved of great value to the Society.

Signed on behalf of the Members of the Society.

President.

Hon. Secretary.

York.   April 10th 1922.

1872
1922

Pl. 14.   A testimonial presented to the Sub-Curator William Watson in recognition of 50 years service to the Society

115

Geological Survey Museum, and J. W. Jackson, of Manchester Museum), Council appointed Walter Edward Collinge.

Walter Edward Collinge (1867-1947)

Walter Collinge, D.Sc., was born in Huddersfield, and educated in Liverpool, at the Yorkshire College in Leeds (now Leeds University) and at the Universities of Edinburgh and St. Andrews. In 1895 he was awarded the Darwin Gold Medal, and in 1916-1919 held a Carnegie Fellowship. For a while he was a lecturer in Zoology and Comparative Anatomy at the University of Birmingham, where he first looked after the departmental museum, and later established a Museum of Economic Biology. He was the founder and editor of the *Journal of Economic Biology*. He then became a Research Fellow at St. Andrews, where he was also assistant to the Director of the University Museum of Natural History.

His particular interests were in natural history and especially ornithology, and he was a member of the Government Wild Bird Advisory Committee (Scotland).

Collinge was clearly an efficient and experienced organiser, and while at York he played an active part in many of the local scientific societies, and acted as local secretary for many visiting scientific conferences. He was a voluminous writer, both for scientific journals and the local press, and organised educational tours of the Museum and 'lecturettes', as well as providing new displays in the Museum, and adding important material to the natural history collections. The *Yorkshire Gazette* claimed that on his retirement at the age of 72, in 1940, he:

'found a society in poor financial conditions, and an understaffed and neglected Museum. As a scientist of more than European fame, he quickly raised the prestige of the Society, and as an able and experienced museum administrator and organiser the Museum rose to be one of the finest in the province . . .'

This improvement (somewhat overstated) was however mainly cosmetic. The real problems of the Society lay in the maintenance of the stored material, as Collinge pointed out in a report to Council soon after his appointment:

'It is at once evident that owing to a variety of causes (such as the late war and the absence of a Keeper) conditions have arisen which if allowed to continue will seriously mitigate against the usefulness and scientific activity of the Museum.

'I refer more particularly to the lack of co-ordination and registration which must at once be taken in hand . . . the absence of a chronological acquisitional record, a card catalogue and strict numerical tabulation of all specimens should at once be remedied . . . the collections have to a large extent outgrown the present building.'

This report was written only a month after Collinge took office, and it is doubtful whether he could, in such a short time, have completely realised the extent of the problem – in the geology department alone over 100,000 specimens were uncatalogued.

Collinge's 'front of house' activities – lectures, displays, articles, and his ornithological interest – could have left him with little time to personally catalogue any of the collections, so this continued to be in the hands of the assistant staff, mainly Mr. Watson, and the Honorary Curators.

William Watson's duties included all the general Caretaker/Attendant duties of the Museum, as well as acting as general dogsbody to the Honorary Curators. His particular interest was photography, and he proved a highly skilled darkroom technician. The additional tasks which Watson was given indicate the extent to which the Council had lost touch with the size of their collection:

'Mr. Watson is capable of carrying out . . . under the Keeper's Supervision, the partial relabelling of the Geological and Palaeontological Collections . . . he shall catalogue and number the whole of the Tempest Anderson Collection of Lantern Slides, as far as possible, in order that a card catalogue may be prepared . . .'

(May 1925)

No attempt was made to number or catalogue the palaeontological material, nor did Watson manage to tackle the smaller task of the Tempest Anderson photographs, not surprisingly, as this collection of some 10,000 negatives and slides more recently took almost two years of full-time effort to catalogue.

Johnson had by now retired to Ripon, and evidently was rarely seen at the Museum, as in March 1924 Council considered the desirability of an Honorary Curator in Geology – and within a month were writing to Johnson with their apologies, and assuring him they meant no criticism of his work for the department.

By now the acquisition of specimens for the geology department had slowed down, in contrast to other sections, particularly that of archaeology, where the redevelopment of city centre sites was providing an increasing flow of material into the Museum. In most years the annual report is able to mention some cleaning and rearranging work carried out on the geological material, and the report for 1926 states that a catalogue of Types is badly needed, with no reference to Platnauer's 1890 and 1894 publications.

This call for help was answered by Sidney Melmore (1884-1969) an amateur geologist of independent means, who had moved to York from Cumberland. Melmore was to publish several short scientific papers on specimens in the Museum's collections and other geological topics, but his main interest, as a field geologist, was the glacial topography of the Vale of York, and he is perhaps best known for his book *The Glacial Geology of Holderness and the Vale of York* which was published in 1935.

Melmore started working on the Type and Figured specimens in 1927, and in 1928 was elected Honorary Curator of Geology. In the next couple of years he brought together in adjacent cases all the specimens figured by John Phillips, and all the other Type and Figured specimens, as far as he could, and compiled a catalogue, although the latter was not published until 1945.

During this time an attempt was made to start a subscription – the 'Million Shilling Fund' – to build a grand new Museum to replace the present building. Not surprisingly Northern England during the depression proved barren ground, and the subscription was soon closed with only a few pounds to show. It was obvious that the Society was going to have to manage with the restricted facilities of the old building, which by now was approaching its centenary, and was beginning to need major expenditure on maintenance.

In 1930 the Hospitium – the timbered mediaeval building used to house archaeological material – needed major repairs and part of the contents were transferred to one of the geology galleries, preventing access to the Yorkshire Fossil collection. This started off a general round of disruption as Melmore, conscious of the importance of the Yorkshire material, moved it into the Tertiary room; the Pleistocene fossils from the Reed collection were placed in the small room which already housed the Kirkdale Cave, Bielsbeck and Sewerby material.

While Collinge attempted to brighten up the galleries with displays of more interest to the general public, Melmore was becoming concerned about the neglect of the scientific aspect of the collections, which, as he pointed out, formed the basis of the Museum. He was to write of these times to a later Keeper, Mr. Willmot, 'the attitude of the Council towards the geological collections was one of complete indifference born of *total ignorance*.' (7th November 1951). Collinge, by now well into his 60's, retreated more and more into contemplation of his entomological collections, and Melmore's frustration led him to resign the position of Honorary Curator of Geology more than once; the Council's indifference cannot have been so complete, as they persuaded him each time to reconsider his resignation. On at least one occasion this resignation seems to have been brought about by some difference of opinion between himself and Collinge, and the Council had to record that 'the Keeper is not entitled to call for a motion of censure upon a member of Council . . .'

118

This unhappy state cannot be correlated with a lack of public interest in the science of geology at this time. Melmore's obituarist recalls 'memories of a small group of keen amateur geologists who flourished in the 1930's in York', and competent professional geologists were on hand, as the North-East Regional Office of the Geological Survey was based in York 1925-1938. The latter included C. N. Bromehead, who had applied for the post of Keeper in 1921, and who for a brief period in 1928-1929 became an Honorary Curator of Geology with Melmore. Sadly it seems probable that the problems which so frustrated Melmore drove away Bromehead and other younger geologists, thus widening the gap between Council and the collections.

One scientist who did persist with the collections was W. J. Arkell, then of Oxford University Museum, who, from 1926 onwards, made great use of the Yorkshire Museum's superb collections of Yorkshire Jurassic fossils in his classic work on Jurassic lamellibranchs and ammonites. He visited the Museum on several occasions, and loans of material were made to him by Melmore and Collinge, although the latter evidently complained when Arkell acknowledged Melmore's help in one of his papers, Collinge pointing out that loans were his responsibility. Arkell encouraged Collinge to improve the display of the ammonite collections, but was later dismayed by worsening conditions at the Museum; Dr. R. Casey of the Geological Survey recalls Arkell returning from a visit to York in the 1940's and reporting that the fossil collections were being thrown out.

CHAPTER 8

Into Public Ownership (1940-1970)

DURING THE 1939-1945 WAR YORK suffered few air raids, but during the 'Baedeker' raid of April 1942, the Museum only narrowly missed destruction. In September 1939 Council, prompted by Melmore, discussed whether to remove the geological type specimens to the basement, but decided to leave them in their cases, to be protected by boards when necessary. In early 1940 Melmore again suggested their removal to the basement, but the Post Office commandeered this area, especially the 'old kitchen' beneath the Central Hall, and the old laboratory at the base of the stairs, to use as a communications centre, so that specimens already stored in these areas had to be moved elsewhere. In October 1941 and January 1942 'valuable specimens' were removed to several locations in the Lake District for safety.

Collinge had retired in 1940, at the age of 72, and it was decided to appoint a new Keeper for the duration of the war only; in January 1941 Reginald Wagstaffe was appointed. Wagstaffe, then Curator of the Municipal Museum at Stockport, had previously gained experience at Liverpool and Leicester, and had also spent a year and a half at the University of Cincinatti, Ohio. His outstanding abilities were in the fields of ornithology and taxidermy.

One witness of this period was Dr. G. F. Elliot, of the B.M. (N.H.). Dr. Elliot had worked at the British Museum for several years before joining the army during the war, and upon finding himself posted to Fulford Barracks, York, during 1942/43, volunteered to assist the Museum during his spare time, working with Melmore and Wagstaffe on the collections. He remembers both Melmore and Wagstaffe as practical, sensible Curators, but working under an overwhelming burden of a backlog of curatorial problems; Wagstaffe, who lived with his wife in Manor Cottage next to the Museum, often worked late into the night, to the

120

detriment of his health. Collinge had done little work on the collections for several years, and emergency treatment with paraffin wax was necessary for many of the Oxford Clay fossils, which were breaking up. On the 'Baedeker' raid of 29th April 1942 a string of bombs fell across the centre of York, the worst destruction being that of the Guildhall, which was completely burnt out. One bomb only just missed the Museum, landing in the ruins of St. Mary's Abbey and causing considerable damage to the roof and windows of the Museum. Dr. Elliot, Wagstaffe and the young daughter of one of the Museum staff cleared up the wreckage, salvaging Type fossils and anything of obvious value from the debris, but 'seven large bath-tubs' of broken glass, fossils, etc. had to be thrown out.

(Recent excavation for a car-park at the back of the Museum revealed a deposit of fossils, bone, antlers and debris, liberally laced with splinters of glass. Some of the fossils were beyond salvation, but over 100 were reincorporated into the collections.)

No attempt seems to have been made to replace Melmore when he finally retired, due partly to failing eyesight, in 1945, and in other departments Honorary Curators seem to have been appointed to whatever subject or portion of a subject caught their fancy, so that for short periods there might be a report from the Curator of Silver Plate and Pewter, or the Curator of Arachnology. Most of these Curators were elderly gentlemen; immersed in their tiny corners of the Museum's by now vast collections, they had little concern for the state of the Museum as a whole, yet they still formed the body to which the Keeper and staff were responsible. Within this ageing body there was a group of younger enthusiasts; in particular mention should be made of Mary Kitson Clark (now Mrs. Derwas Chitty) who was appointed Honorary Curator of Roman Antiquities in 1942. This was extended to include Ethnology the next year, and for the next 10 years, until her marriage and removal from York, Miss Kitson Clark not only organised and catalogued much of the Museum's archaeological collections but also arranged lectures and exhibitions on many aspects of archaeology, history and the cultural arts. E. Wilfred Taylor (1891-1980) who had a lifetime's association with the Society, and became Curator of Vertebrate Zoology in 1943, and W. D. Hincks, who was the Honorary Curator of Entomology (excluding Lepidoptera) also from 1943, sounded warning notes in the published Annual Reports as to the state of the collections.

The most noteworthy feature of this decade is the degree of optimism expressed in the Annual Report. In 1943 Council wished to extend the Society's educational work, and Wagstaffe was asked to prepare a report on 'The future possibilities of the Society and its Museums'. This was

121

considered 'in relation to the proposed review of the cultural and educational activities which the Corporation is undertaking', and was then referred to the Honorary Curators for discussion and emendation. By 1944 Council reported to the members that it had drawn up a scheme, with the co-operation of the Keeper and Honorary Curators. This 'Report of the Cultural Aims of the Yorkshire Philosophical Society' is difficult to reconcile with the actual state of the Museum and its collections at that time. It implies an institution with well-ordered collections, adequately stored and catalogued, and an abundance of staff and money.

The explanation for these noble aims may be found in the educational movement then afoot in York. Before the war, in 1935 John Bowes Morrell, an elder statesman of York, had, in *City of our Dreams*, revived the old idea of an University in York, and with the Dean of York, Oliver Sheldon, and Noel Terry, directors of the two influential chocolate firms of York, founded the Civic Trust in 1946. This led to the York Academic Trust and ultimately to the founding of York University in 1953.

The relevance of this movement to the proposed educational role of the Yorkshire Museum becomes clearer when we note that Morrell (who was a Director of Rowntree, Chairman of the Westminster Press, and Lord Mayor of York in 1914/15, and again in 1949/50) was on the Council and the General Purposes and Finance Committee of the Y.P.S.; Oliver Sheldon was a Council Member, and Sir Francis Terry (Noel Terry's grandfather and Co-Director), was a Trustee, Vice-President and member of the G.P. and F. Committee.

That the Yorkshire Philosophical Society should have been deeply involved in the movement for educational change is appropriate, but unfortunately these politically minded members of Council had little concept of the size and extent of the internal problems by now facing the Museum. By 1946 the Society was congratulating itself on its prosperous financial position, which had enabled it to appoint a professional archaeologist (Dudley Waterman) and to install a new laboratory and dark-room. This was followed by the appointment of a natural history assistant (Mr. Williamson), and the next year saw the following announcement in the Annual Report:

'The possession of this well-equipped and up-to-date laboratory has placed us in what is probably a unique position among provincial museums in this country, in so far as we can not only carry out all types of preparatory work with the maximum speed and efficiency and minimum expense, but can also offer *bona fide* students of museum methods and technique splendid facilities for a first-class training.'

By the end of 1947 the Museum Committee was able to report to the Council on the reorganisation of the Museum:

122

'Much unseen work has also gone to the removal of type and other collections to the basement as a necessary preliminary to the rearrangement of other galleries . . . an additional assistant is suggested for two years work on the arrangement in storage of the geological collections . . . Geological Room. That this room become the Botanical Room for the time being, the geological specimens to be covered . . . Saurian Room to remain as it is for the time being. Kirkdale Cave Room be curtained off until such time as the Keeper is able to deal with this room.'

By now there was no Honorary Curator of Geology to speak up for his subjects, but it must be noted that, while the *fossils* were to be banished from the galleries, the subject of *geology* was not. Although the main geology gallery and all the upper balcony galleries were lost to the subject, the Saurian gallery (half of which was occupied by the three giant fossils) and the old bird gallery were redisplayed during the early 1950's with geological models illustrating the latest geological theories, complete with light bulbs that lit up at the touch of a button, and small 'dioramas', illustrating life in the seas during 'The Age of Mud' as the Silurian was labelled, or 'The Age of Dinosaurs'. But of the many thousands of fine and rare fossils which had been on display, less than 200 remained, and their role was to demonstrate the common-place. Much of this work was carried out with the help of two young temporary assistants, Geoffrey Watson (now Chief Recreation and Amenities Officer with the Middlesbrough Recreation and Amentities Department) and Anthony Tynan (now Curator of the Hancock Museum, University of Newcastle upon Tyne).

The extent to which the Museum was courting the favours of the public in its galleries is revealed by the following paragraph, also from the Annual Report for 1946, published in 1947:

'an aquarium . . . in . . . a large room in the basement . . . it requires little imagination to appreciate the great potentialities of such an exhibition. A well-stocked Aquarium would not only extend our educational services to the City, materially helping the Society to achieve its highest aspirations for the betterment of its cultural life, but it would also prove a financial asset of considerable magnitude, and might well become the wage-earner for the further reconstruction of other important departments.'

There was no place in such a display philosophy for cases of fossils. The term 'dusty fossil' has long been a cliché standing for all that is unappetising and outdated in the museum world, and the Yorkshire Museum's fossils were not only suffering from 100 years of exposure to the York atmosphere, which until recently was heavily charged with pollutants from the industrial West Riding; they also had to contend with an architectural peculiarity of the Museum building. Vents from the original unsatisfactory heating system led air directly from the boiler room to every part of the building; this air was heavily contaminated with coal dust from the daily task of stoking the boiler. Thus everything in the Museum was covered with a black dust, which sank into the pores of the stone until all the fossils, whatever their matrix, presented an dark grey appearance with all fine detail obscured.

It took almost 10 years to transfer all the geological material to store, the process being completed by Wagstaffe's successor George Willmot. It soon became evident that there was little room in the basement, and so the upper balcony display areas were closed to the public and the cases used for storage. The fossils were packed into an assortment of secondhand boxes acquired from local shops, and labelled on the outside with a vague indication of their contents. As there was no catalogue of the collection, this effectively removed the material from the reach of any but the most dedicated researcher, who would be faced with some two to three thousand boxes, piled up to ceiling height in dirty cases on a narrow, unlit balcony.

The majority of the fossils had been displayed in stratigraphical order, and this tended to be retained as the material was stored away, but as this process was carried out over so many years, as other work allowed, inevitably material did get out of place. Fortunately the foresight of Charlesworth, Reed and Walker, in fastening the specimens to labelled boards and providing pill-boxes for many of the fragile shells, in the previous century, minimised damage to the specimens.

By early 1948 the 'prosperous financial position' of the previous year had evaporated, and the Society was again seeking ways of raising money. When Mr. Williamson, the biologist, left in February he was not replaced, and by July Council were considering an application to the Carnegie Trust for a grant to convert the Geological Gallery into an Invertebrate Room.

On 12th December 1949 Council heard that the Carnegie Trust was unwilling to help because the Chairman of a joint committee with the Museums Association was 'greatly perturbed about the position at York'.

As Council held the Keeper to be responsible to them for the Museum, they called Wagstaffe to a special meeting the next week, at which he was asked to resign. The post was advertised at a salary of £500 plus free accommodation, but the person appointed on 6th March 1950 was found to have falsified much of his application, and on 13th March it was decided to readvertise the post at a higher salary.

Meanwhile criticism was being heard from the members about Council's treatment of Wagstaffe, and alternative candidates for Council to those nominated by the outgoing Council were proposed at the A.G.M. on 17th April. The normal order of the meeting was reversed, votes being counted before the discussion, so that the press could be excluded from the latter, at the suggestion of the President the Earl of Scarborough, as:

'matters in dispute contained quite substantial domestic and personal elements among them. Charges were likely to be made, and if made answered, and in the process things might be said which might be damaging to the Society.'

The Council's nominees were returned with a large majority; of the subsequent discussion the minutes of the meeting merely record:

'. . . some misunderstanding existed among members of the Society with regard to the Council's plans for the future of the Museum and the rearrangement of the collections. Various questions raised . . . were answered . . .'

George Francis Willmot (1908-1977)

In May 1950 Mr. G. F. Willmot (pl. 15) was appointed to the post of Keeper. Willmot was the son of a Bournemouth solicitor, and made his first important archaeological discovery, an Anglo-Saxon burial ground at Abington, in Berkshire, at the age of 19. He read English at Oxford, and became a teacher, first in Bedford and then at the Roman Catholic Ampleforth College, north of York. There he began to study the archaeology of Yorkshire, and first made contact with the Yorkshire Museum.

During the war Willmot was a commissioned officer in the infantry. He then joined the Monuments, Fine Arts and Antiquities branch of the Control Commission for Germany, helping to trace works of art and antiquity taken by the Germans from occupied countries, and for a period was in charge of the Fine Arts Repository at Schloss Celle. Following this he spent some time excavating archaeological sites in Jersey, until his appointment to the Yorkshire Museum.

Willmot was widely acknowledged to be a brilliant archaeologist, but published little about either his many excavations or the results of his pioneering work on the Bronze Age Beaker cultures.

He brought to the post of Keeper a personality which combined the attacking spirit of a military strategist with a sharp legal mind. Respected by archaeologists and museum professionals for his knowledge, which extended beyond traditional museum subjects to a fine grasp of the details of such subjects as committee procedure and legal responsibilities, he spoke several European languages. Willmot enjoyed a fight, which for him was a form of mental exercise, but unfortunately would vigorously attack individuals as well as their policies, ultimately isolating the Museum from many researchers and helpers.

Pl. 15.   George Willmot working in the Museum, 1966

In addition to initiating archaeological excavations in St. Mary's Abbey, and working on the redisplay of the Bird Gallery, Willmot took over from Wagstaffe the task of placing the geological collections in storage and supervising the setting up of new archaeological displays. He was worried by the state of the material, especially the Type and Figured specimens, and reported the situation to Council early in 1951. He also wrote to Sydney Melmore:

'In the old kitchen was an enormous mass of loose bones – remains of certain parts of the Allis collection. When I had got this cleared, I found behind it a pile of what I took to be waste-packing paper. On investigating it I found that it was waste packing paper and many of the type fossils. Some of the fossils are broken and practically all are adrift from their cards . . . What has happened is that the fossils came back from their storage place, somebody needed a packing case, and the whole lot were just pitched out on the floor and left for several years. I have done my best to sort out the pile, but I cannot undertake to marry up the fossils and the mounting cards. It needs a palaeontologist.'

Melmore was saddened by this information, as he had carefully packed the fossils away, recording the contents of each box in an exercise book (which had also been lost). However, failing eyesight meant that he could no longer help, and he urged Willmot to bring in outside assistance. By July the latter could report that quite a number of the Type fossils had been sorted out by Mr. J. A. Dell. John Alexander Dell was a Zoology Graduate of Durham University who had been Biology Master at Bootham School in York from 1912-1942, and a Council member of the Yorkshire Geological Society.

Towards the end of 1951 Willmot received an approach, *via* Dr. Dorothy Rayner at Leeds University, to the effect that the British Museum (Natural History) might be interested in buying the Type and Figured material from the collections. By November they had made an unofficial offer for the Type and Figured specimens, as listed in Melmore's catalogue, and all the non-Yorkshire fossils.

Although Willmot was in favour of some important material, especially the skeleton of the Moa, *Dinornis robustus*, going down to London, he was concerned about the ethics of splitting the collection in this way, and rightly so, as recent research has identified some 400 further Type and Figured specimens among the collections, some of which had been presumed 'lost' since the death of their original collector.

This suggestion opened the way for further consideration of the future of the collection independently of the Yorkshire Museum, and Willmot then wrote to Dr. J. E. Hemingway, also of Leeds University, and Secretary of the Yorkshire Geological Society, pointing out that while the Y.P.S. had the specimens the Y.G.S. had the geologists, and hoping that it might be possible to come to some arrangement to set up a Museum of Yorkshire Geology. This was not a practical idea, as the Y.G.S. had even less financial backing than the Y.P.S., but by November 1952 the idea had germinated of passing the whole collection over to Leeds University on permanent loan, to be displayed in the University buildings, the suggestion being that the Y.P.S., the Y.G.S. and Leeds University should be trustees of a new Yorkshire Geological Museum, which would be staffed and administered by the University, and would be open to the public.

This was considered in detail by the University's administrators during 1953, but sufficient funds could not be found for the necessary building and staff provision.

Willmot's vigorous approach to the Museum's problems angered those Honorary Curators and Council Members who felt that the Keeper should be subservient to their wishes. In May 1953 the Council Minutes record an acrimonious discussion between the Keeper and Council, and by January 1954 the situation had worsened to the point where Willmot's resignation was requested, and a decision was taken to approach York Corporation to ask for their assistance in running the Museum and Gardens.

Memories of the A.G.M. which followed Wagstaffe's 'resignation' only four years previously were still fresh in the minds of those who felt the Keeper was being blamed unfairly for a situation beyond his control, and they called for a Special Meeting, which was held on 8th March. After Council had explained that the background to their action was '[the Keeper's] failure to respect the authority of his employing body' and Willmot had read a statement in reply, the members asked for his report on the state of the Museum, which had been presented, to Council only, early in 1951, to be read out to them. After a long discussion a resolution, instructing Council to request the Keeper to withdraw his resignation, was passed by a large majority.

At the A.G.M. all the Council's nominations for offices were successfully opposed. The old Council, with its two titled gentlemen, three Lieutenant-Colonels, and liberal sprinkling of D.S.O.'s, O.B.E.'s, etc. was replaced by a group of younger people with a practical interest in the Museum, with an emphasis on archaeologists, including T. C. M. Brewster, L. P. Wenham, and Miss E. Brunskill. Both the entomologist Arthur Smith and botanist Miss C. M. Rob, who had been on the old committee, were elected Vice-Presidents, Miss Rob also took over the central position of Honorary Secretary to the Society.

Thus the governing body of the Society was brought back to seeing as its main duty the management of the Museum. The Honorary Curators were not re-elected, and for the first time in the Museum's history the relationship between the Keeper and Council was placed on a fully professional basis.

By now all the geological material had been consigned to storage, and, being out of sight, was largely forgotten. Although material was on occasion made available to research workers, the lack of any catalogue and shortage of staff meant that research use of the collections was hardly encouraged. One of the saddest casualties of this period was the skeleton of the Irish Elk, one of the most famous of the Museum's geological specimens. This had been the first *Megaceros* skeleton displayed in an English museum, in 1836; mounted under John Phillip's supervision, it was acknowledged to be a particularly fine specimen. As its base was required for an aquarium display the skeleton was consigned, together with other, recent skeletal material, to totally inadequate storage in the changing huts surrounding the disused swimming pool. Decay and vandalism soon reduced both the fabric of these crude buildings and their contents into a heap of rubble and bones in the swimming pool, which was infilled and grassed over in the early 1970's.

The new Council was concerned about the long-term future of the Museum. Since the 1920's, year after year, expenditure on the Museum had been considerably greater than income. The difference had been made up from the Society's capital, which was essentially that bequeathed by Dr. Tempest Anderson in 1913. It was obvious that rising costs could not forever be met out of the decreasing capital base, and by 1955, in an attempt to contain the problem, staffing had been reduced to the bare minimum, with only the Keeper and a handyman to look after the Museum and collections. A further financial blow fell when the Society failed to persuade the Rating Authorities of the charitable status of the Museum.

Several grants from the Carnegie Trust during this period helped with improvements to the displays, in particular the creation of a new Roman Gallery in what had been the Geology Gallery, but, opening this new feature, in 1958, Professor Ian Richmond said that 'he could not look upon himself so much as a skeleton at the feast as somebody providing a feast to a Society reduced almost to a skeleton'.

In the same year the Society voted to raise the membership subscriptions, for the first time in its history, from the 1822 level of two pounds to three guineas (£3.15p). The original subscription had been set at a level attractive, in 1822, to the wealthier citizens of the county, the intellectuals and philosophers among the landed gentry, doctors, clergymen and other professional men. The fact that the subscription was not increased over the years reflected the extent to which the Society,

129

financially cushioned, from 1913, by the Tempest Anderson bequest, was opening its embrace to the ordinary wage-earner. Even so, it is surprising that some adjustment had not already been made during the inflationary post-war years of the 20th century.

Negotiations with the City in 1957 had centred round suggestions that the Gardens should be leased to the City, releasing the Society from the cost of their upkeep. However it was realised that the 100,000 visitors who paid to enter the Gardens each year came to see the St. Mary's Abbey ruins and the mediaeval Hospitium as well as the Museum, or simply to enjoy the pleasures of the riverside gardens, and the Museum alone could not rely on a similar number of paying visitors.

By the end of 1959 an agreement had been drawn up between the York Corporation and the Society, under which the Society agreed to hand over 'the Museum, the Collections and the Gardens' to the City. The Society was to be represented on the new Committee, and was to make grants in aid towards the Museum.

After a further year during which the details of the agreement were worked out, the Museum and the Gardens were formally handed over to the City on 2nd January 1961 by Sir Herbert Read, the President of the Society, who ended his speech by saying:

'I believe that in the new age we are entering today, both the Yorkshire Philosophical Society and the Yorkshire Museum will be free to develop to the full their separate interests. The Society will resume with new energies its proper business, which is the promotion of natural science and the study of archaeology and antiquities, both fields in which there is a vast amount of work to be done. Whereas the Museum, with the aid and enthusiasm of its new owners, the Lord Mayor, Aldermen and Citizens of the City of York, could become a centre of attraction for visitors from all over this county, this country and indeed from all countries in the world. My Lord Mayor, Aldermen and Councillors, we, the members of this Society, are giving away great possessions, but giving them in the certain knowledge that you will use them for the general benefit of the people.'

The immediate effect on the Society was severe. As the Museum and Gardens were now open to all, one of the prized benefits of membership was lost. During 1950-57 the membership had been stable at around 450. For the next three years it had decreased at the rate of 50 members each year, until in 1960 it stood at 300; by 1962, as the Society worried about its new role, it had plunged to 125.

In April 1965 the Society staff moved from the office they had retained in the Museum to the Lodge at the main entrance to the Gardens, offered by York City Council at a peppercorn rent. Here the Society was able to settle into its new situation, with stated aims of encouraging and publishing local research, and engaging leading scientists to lecture both to the Society members and to specially organised school groups.

By the end of that year the Society had gained 48 new members, and the Annual Report sounded a more confident note. Twenty years later, with a membership of over 600, the Society continues to provide financial assistance to the Museum, and four members sit on the Museum sub-committee.

For the first three years of ownership York Corporation proceeded more slowly than had been hoped with its promise of more staff for the Museum.

In 1960, as negotiations with the City were proceeding, the British Museum (Natural History) had approached the Town Clerk to suggest that the Type and Figured geological material should be transferred to the national museum. Early in 1963 the Standing Commission on Museums and Galleries published a *Survey of Provincial Museums and Galleries*, in which specific mention was made of the Yorkshire Museum on p. 23, para. 70. While most of this paragraph, which details the hazards which can destroy type specimen collections which remain in provincial museums, is of a general nature, York was included in the long list of museums referred to. More seriously, the Yorkshire Museum was singled out for special mention '. . . The York collection has been ruined by pyritization'. This statement, whether it is meant to refer to the whole collection or only the type material, is patently untrue; indeed, only some of the fossils are preserved in a pyrite-rich matrix and therefore susceptible to pyrite decay, and of these the majority were, and still are, in good condition.

For an expert opinion Willmot turned again to Prof. Hemingway, who confirmed that the collection was in good condition, adding 'It would indeed be interesting to know on what evidence the statement is made that the Yorkshire collection has been ruined by pyritisation. This can only be regarded as a monstrous mis-statement.' The letter continues with a strong argument for the retention of type collections in the larger local museums, where they are near to their source rocks, and to the centre of research on these rocks 'assuming the continuity of good curatorship which in the case of the Yorkshire Museum is not in doubt . . .'

Armed with this latest attack on the Museum, the committee once again pressed for staff, and in April 1964 the appointment of a geologist, geological technician, biologist and biological technician were approved.

Colin Simms was appointed as the biologist at the end of 1964, but advertisements for the post of geologist brought a poor response; twice

131

suitably qualified candidates withdrew before appointment, and Willmot's hospitalisation for several weeks at the end of 1964 also delayed matters.

Finally an Indian geologist, Udaysingh Madhavrao Bagwe, was appointed in September 1965; he had a B.Sc. and a Diploma in Museology, apparently from Baroda University. He had spent one and a half years as a gallery assistant in the Salar Jung National Museum, Hyderabad, and had no previous first-hand knowledge of British geology or palaeontology, but he was willing to come to grips with the central problem of the collection at that time, the accumulated dirt and general chaos; it is said that he wore out a vacuum cleaner within a couple of years. When he was appointed he was shown into the basement geology store-room and work-room by candlelight; three years later the room was clean and adequately, if not well lit, several cabinets containing geological material had been cleaned and repaired, moved in or near to this room, numbered, and their contents had been briefly noted.

In 1967 Bagwe appealled, via the local press, for voluntary assistance with the collections. This was answered by Dr. Stanley Underwood, the recently retired Medical Officer of Rowntrees & Co. Ltd., the confectionary manufacturers. Dr. Underwood had originally taken a degree in mining geology, then turned to the medical profession for a career, on the advice of his father. He was now attracted by the idea of exploring the field of palaeontology, rather than his old interest of mineralogy, and could bring to the Museum a background of geology and biology, plus a strong streak of practicality.

Dr. Underwood was in many ways the perfect museum volunteer. He came without any preconceived notions as to what was required of him, or any over-riding interest in any one section of the collections, and offered to help with whatever was necessary. For the next 10 years he spent one or two half days each week on the basic curatorial task of unwrapping the specimens from their newspaper, cleaning them of the accumulated dirt, classifying them into major zoological and stratigraphical groups, and typing out lists as he replaced them in store in clean boxes. In this way he listed almost all the collection, an estimated 150,000 specimens, and became probably the first person since Miss Holmes at the beginning of the century to examine the whole of the geological collections of the Museum. His wisdom and maturity, coupled with a perfect 'bedside manner', also proved of value within the department, as the Museum struggled to define its role under the new management of local government.

Bagwe left, after three years, to take up a post in Canada, and I took up the post of Keeper of Geology in September 1968.

132

Willmot had already suffered two periods of severe illness while at York, and early in 1969 suffered a stroke from which he never fully recovered. He retired in January 1970, but kept in daily contact with the Museum until his death in 1977.

His successor, appointed in 1970, was Allen Butterworth (1939-1974). Born at Stockport in Cheshire, he studied Latin, Greek and Romano-British Archaeology at Leeds University, after which he took a diploma in Prehistoric European Archaeology at the Institute of Archaeology in London. He worked at Leicester Museums and then at Sheffield City Museums, where he rose to the position of Deputy Director, before moving to York.

In 1971 he revived the practice of publishing a detailed report on each department of the Museum in the Annual Report of the Y.P.S. (who maintain their office in The Lodge in the Museum Gardens) so that the history of the Museum during the last few years and hopefully into the future, is readily accessible.

CHAPTER 9

A Modern Museum (1970-1988)

IN CONSIDERING THE LAST 20 YEARS, the emphasis obviously moves from historical research into the area of personal experience. This chapter can be little more than a résumé of events; so much has happened both in the Museum and indeed in York itself, as the City has adapted to life in the post-industrial era of leisure industries.

Once York Corporation had tackled major structural problems within the building – in particular replacing the roof over the Central Hall and restoring the fine carved plasterwork ceiling, and taking steps to eliminate death watch beetle in the Hospitium – they were able to start updating the galleries, which were still furnished in general with the original cases, now over 100 years old and showing signs of wear.

The Saurian Gallery was the first to be completely stripped back to the walls. This was rebuilt as two display areas, a small room with exhibits from Kirkdale Cave and a larger gallery displaying to the best advantage the two large Jurassic sea-reptiles mounted onto the wall over 100 years earlier. Two large diorama cases were incorporated into the gallery, one of which provides a fishy home for a life-size Jurassic ichthyosaur modelled out of glass-fibre and resin. A 'Fossil Wall' extended from the new gallery into the Square Geology Gallery; around 150 fossils, mounted into the wall in resin blocks, could be handled by visitors. This proved a great attraction, particularly to our younger visitors.

The decision was also taken, at the end of 1971, to introduce admission charges for visitors, although York residents and Y.P.S. members were still admitted free; the revenue was to help offset the cost of improvements to the galleries. This meant that an accurate count of visitors was taken for the first time, and in 1972 98,000 people came to the Museum.

Meanwhile the subject of archaeology in York was undergoing a revival. For many years excavation and recording of archaeological sites in York had been undertaken on a personal, voluntary basis by several individuals and groups, with between them a wealth of experience and qualification but with no official status or permanent backing (apart from the York Minster archaeological team). Growing concern at the scale of redevelopment in the centre of the City, which included proposals for a major inner ring road to skirt the City Walls, prompted the Y.P.S. to join forces with the Council for British Archaeology, as a result of which the York Archaeological Trust for Excavation and Research was set up in April 1972.

Allen Butterworth became the first Secretary of the Y.A.T., and with its Director, Peter V. Addyman, worked tirelessly to establish what rapidly became one of the country's leading rescue archaeology organisations. A Keeper of Archaeology, Miss Elizabeth Blank (now Mrs. Hartley), had been appointed to the Museum staff in 1971 ; one of her main tasks was to be coping with the quantities of material excavated by the Trust and passed on to the Museum for safe-keeping.

Allen Butterworth planned the complete redevelopment of the Museum, but sadly was unable to do more than initiate a Schools Loan Service and draw up plans for the refurbishment of the Central Hall before his death, at the tragically early age of 35, in 1974.

1974 was also marked by the reorganisation of Local Government Authorities. York Corporation had been independent of the three Ridings of Yorkshire ; under the new arrangements the region of Yorkshire was split into four, and York became a City within the new North Yorkshire County Council. York City Council retained the Castle Museum and the Art Gallery, but the Yorkshire Museum was passed, with the approval of the Philosophical Society as a Trustee, to the N.Y.C.C., where it came under the Libraries, Museums and Archives Committee. In order to accommodate the requirements of the Trust Deeds, and to provide an adequate forum for the discussion of the special requirements of a museum, a Museum Sub-Committee was created, onto which the Y.P.S. nominate representatives.

The Yorkshire Museum thus became the County Museum of North Yorkshire, with the responsibility of providing advice and assistance to both public and private museums within the county, when requested. In this role the Museum, and particularly the Curator, has been closely involved with the existing museums at Malton, Whitby and Pickering, and more recently with the new Yorkshire Museum of Farming at Murton and the Yorkshire Aircraft Museum at Elvington. It is interesting to note that all these museums, founded and owned by local societies and manned almost entirely by volunteers, represent the continuation to the present day of the spirit which initiated the Yorkshire Museum over 150 years ago.

Thomas Michael Clegg (pl. 16) was appointed to the position of Keeper (now renamed Curator) in the autumn of 1974. He was born in Barnsley, that stronghold of Yorkshire tradition, and started his career under Professor Krebs (a familiar name to all biochemistry students). He worked in several Yorkshire museums before moving for a while to Dundee, where he was Depute Curator of the Museums and Art Galleries.

A biologist by training, Michael Clegg's involvement encompassed other, related fields of interest; thus in the Orkneys he studied both the Stone Age settlement of Scara Brae and the population dynamics of the Orkney vole – a plump rodent which he saw as the possible Stone Age version of fast food – and to these added the ability to recite at length from the Viking Sagas.

By the time he came to York he was a successful author and much in demand as a lecturer, and as his broadcasting experience grew, particularly with the Yorkshire Television series 'Clegg's People', it came as no surprise when, after seven eventful years here, he decided to follow a free-lance career.

Under Michael Clegg the rationalisation of the collections continued, with social history material in particular being passed over to the Castle Museum, as it was realised that the future interests of the Museum were best served by the creation of a strong identity as a museum of natural history and archaeology, distinct from other York attractions.

The Museum staff were closely involved with the movement, in the early 1970's, towards the setting up of specialist groups within the museum world, in particular the Geological Curators' Group, the Society for Museum Archaeologists, the Biological Curators' Group, and the Yorkshire and Humberside Collections Research Unit, and as a result of these initiatives became the North Yorkshire centre for Geological and Biological Site Recording. Initial input to these schemes was with the assistance of temporary workers from the Manpower Services Commission, but it was not possible to convert these into permanent jobs, and the sheer size of North Yorkshire – 1,000 geological sites were identified from a literature search alone – has meant that we have fallen behind other museums in this provision.

1976 saw the first in a continuing series of major temporary exhibitions in the Museum. 'The Viking Kingdom of York' was seen by 78,000 visitors, and commemorated the 1,100th anniversary of the founding of Yorvik – modern York – as the capital of the ancient kingdom.

The Museum Gardens had been transferred with the Museum to North Yorkshire County Council. Since 1951 they have periodically been brought to the attention of an international audience as the setting for the York Cycle

Pl. 16. Michael Clegg explains the Fossil Wall to a group of visitors, 1974

137

of Mystery Plays, and on a day-to-day basis still form the 'green lung' for the heart of York and are enjoyed by many shoppers and visitors. However, many of the trees, now one-and-a-half centuries old, were beginning to deteriorate to the point where some were proving dangerous. The Y.P.S. therefore paid for a detailed survey, to identify those which needed immediate surgery and to form the basis for a future management programme.

Arrangements were made whereby the day-to-day care of the Museum Gardens was placed in the hands of the Horticultural Department of the Askham Bryan College of Agriculture, which is also administered by North Yorkshire County Council. This has been mutually beneficial, as students at the College have been able to assist with the planning and creation of new features in the Garden, gaining on-site experience of work in a public area.

In 1976 the Museum was approached for assistance with the creation of a new museum at Hawes, in Upper Wensleydale, to house the extensive Dales Social History collections of Miss Marie Hartley and Miss Joan Ingilby, which they had donated to the North Riding County Council. This was formally instituted as a branch museum of the Yorkshire Museum, and throughout the next two years Michael Clegg and the archaeology technician Peter Hall worked in various stores cataloguing the collections. The process of turning the old engine shed at Hawes Station into the Upper Dales Folk Life Museum coincided with a particularly severe winter – on one Monday morning they had to dig snowdrifts out from inside the building before they could start work.

The Hawes Museum has been a great success, with some 20,000 visitors during the six-month summer opening, but due to its distance from York – some 60 miles – and the subjects covered it has always been seen as a separate entity from the Yorkshire Museum, and more recently a Social Historian has been appointed as a part-time Curator, dividing his time between Hawes and the independently-owned Yorkshire Museum of Farming at Murton.

The summer exhibition programme at the Yorkshire Museum continued with 'A Mammoth Exhibition – the Ice Age in Yorkshire' in 1977, which was visited by over 100,000 visitors in six months. For the first time we received national television coverage as a mammoth tusk from the galleries was featured on 'Blue Peter' only two days before the official opening. The value of this publicity was evident the next day, as we were installing the tusk in place, when a party of young children came in to work in the Roman Gallery. They were amazed to learn that something they had all seen on 'the box' the night before really did exist, although it took the teacher a little while to realise why her party of well-behaved youngsters had stopped in their tracks; she had to promise to bring them in again the next week before they would turn their attention back to the Romans.

The exhibition attracted a wide range of visitors, from pre-school children, fascinated by Hull Museum's large furry mammoth model, to scientists from the Birmingham International Quaternary Conference, and increased the public awareness of the existence of the geology department, with a consequent increase in enquiries and identification requests.

At the same time the image of the department in the research world was being enhanced with the publication of an up-dated Type specimen catalogue (Pyrah, 1976, 1977, 1979), aided by a grant from the Y.P.S. This replaced Melmore's publication of the 1940's, and listed over 900 Type and Figured specimens illustrated in approximately 150 publications. As this information was made available to the scientific world, through the Proceedings of the Yorkshire Geological Society, it resulted in considerable interest from researchers, whose work, studying the specimens, generated more scientific publications to be entered into the catalogue.

Another major research success story was that of the Tempest Anderson collection of photographs. Tempest Anderson, it will be recalled, was the Victorian doctor, vulcanologist and photographer whose collection of photographs, dating from the 1880's to 1913, are preserved in the Museum.

In 1977 the Y.P.S. gave a grant towards a vulcanologist, Dr. R. Suthren, for a preliminary study of this collection to ascertain its scientific value. As a result of his work we received funding from the British Library for the production of a complete catalogue of the 5,000 negatives, which proved to be of considerable importance, covering both volcanic and ethnographical subjects, particularly in the West Indies, the Far East and Northern Europe.

The results of this work, which led to international publicity for the collection, have been much greater than anticipated. Due to the tropical climate of the West Indies few archive records of the 1902 eruption of Soufrière and Mont Pelée have survived there, so our collection of photographs and three volumes of contemporary press cuttings proved of immense interest to the Seismic Research Institute of the University of the West Indies. Details of over 1,000 photographs were requested by the Centre de Volcanologie Vulcain in France, and we were able to help many individual researchers world-wide with relevant material.

The collection has also been of great value to social historians, providing a major contribution to national photographic exhibitions in both Iceland and Norway. In fact, in the 10 years since it has been catalogued, there has been a continuing level of professional interest far greater than we could have anticipated when we first started to investigate the contents of the assorted boxes in which the slides and negatives had been stored since Tempest Anderson's death, and this collection can be seen as a classic example of the potential of provincial museum collections.

In addition to their scientific interest, Anderson's photographs are of superb visual quality, and an exhibition in the Museum in 1978 aroused much public interest, and astounded one elderly visitor from Bournemouth when he found himself looking at a familiar photograph of his mother enjoying deck games on board a ship bound for South Africa in 1910. As his late mother's copy of the photograph had long been lost, we were able to give him a most unusual souvenir of a visit to York.

Meanwhile concern was growing about the storage areas available to the Museum, as finds from the York Archaeological Trust's excavation accumulated. Apart from the limited space in the basement and on the balconies of the main Museum building, material, particularly carved stonework, was stored in several outposts, particularly the old abattoir, a grim building where the main security was provided by the particularly fierce guard dog of a neighbouring trader, while boxes of finds newly excavated by the Trust had to be piled high in the ground floor of the Hospitium in the Museum Gardens.

At the beginning of 1979 major flooding occurred in the Vale of York, the embankment at the foot of the Museum Gardens was inundated and the Hospitium flooded to a depth of several feet. This event underlined the need both for improved flood defences for the Hospitium and for alternative storage accommodation for the collections. An elegant solution to the latter was offered by the Marygate Centre.

In 1862 the Philosophical Society had acquired the lease of an area known as Bearpark's Garden, three acres of the St. Mary's Abbey site in the angle of Marygate and Bootham. After complex negotiations this was taken over by the Yorkshire Fine Art and Industrial Institution for the construction, in 1879, of an exhibition building fronting onto a fine new public square. The building is now owned by York City Council as the City Art Gallery, but Exhibition Square retains its original name.

A large wooden hall behind the main building was demolished in 1941, and a layout of temporary sheds erected to provide space for various departments of the School of Art, which had a suite of rooms in the Art Gallery. With the removal in 1973 of the School of Art and Further Education classes to the Technical College's site at Dringhouses, on the City boundary, this complex, known as the Marygate Centre, was no longer required by the College, and in 1981 negotiations were concluded making the site available to the Museum for storage.

The temporary buildings at Marygate include several rooms large enough for the installation of heavy duty racking with fork-lift access, suitable for the storage of large items of stonework, plus adequate space for shelving to take boxed items. However they are near the end of their life, and plans for a major reconstruction of the area is under consideration. Although the area is not visible from either Exhibition Square or Marygate, it is well situated, with the Abbey walls on one side, the mediaeval buildings of King's Manor on the other, and direct access to the Museum Gardens, and clearly has great potential for sensitive development.

Use of the Marygate Centre relieved the pressure on stores in the main building to a certain degree; in particular, the biology department was able to move out of its extremely cramped, almost tunnel-like conditions under the tiered floor of the Tempest Anderson Hall into a suite of rooms in Marygate, en route for permanent storage in the refurbished St. Mary's Lodge. Considerable improvements were also made in various areas of the main museum stores, with mobile racking for part of the geology collections, and, more recently, the installation of two data protection cabinets for the Type and Figured specimen collection. Unlike ordinary fireproof cabinets these safeguard against both fire and water damage.

The York Archaeological Trust's excavation of the Viking waterfront settlement in Coppergate, brought York, traditionally thought of as a Roman city, to the forefront of Viking studies, and, with similar finds in Dublin and Hedeby, brought the Viking period to the attention of a wider audience. In 1980 the British Museum mounted an International Viking Exhibition, and donated £30,000 to the Yorkshire Museum, to be put towards the costs of providing a permanent gallery to display the Museum's Coppergate material, which is based on finds from previous excavations in the 1930's as well as those discovered by the Trust.

Meanwhile the Trust's work had been arousing great interest in Denmark, and the idea took root of a joint Anglo-Danish exhibition on the Vikings in England, to be shown at Brede and Moesgard, in Denmark, and at the Yorkshire Museum. Kenneth Pearson of the *Sunday Times*, fresh from the success of the Fishbourne Museum, was one of the prime movers, and royal patronage was given by H.M. Queen Margrethe and H.R.H. The Prince of Wales.

'The Vikings in England' was mounted by an independent body, the Anglo-Danish Viking Project, with Peter Addyman of the Trust, Michael Clegg and Dr. David Wilson, the Director of the British Museum, on the English national committee. The Yorkshire Museum lent 350 objects to the exhibition, which was shown at the two Danish venues in 1981 and at York in 1982.

Placing this large travelling exhibition in the confines of the Yorkshire Museum called for considerable adaptation of the existing galleries. In particular the Roman gallery, due for refurbishment, was stripped out – this involved moving almost half the geology collections, which were still stored in what had originally been the geology gallery – and the biology gallery was converted into a shop; the first time the Museum had had a separate sales area apart from the admission desk.

Drawing from the experience of the International Viking Exhibition in London, it was realised that 'The Vikings in England' would be of great educational interest, and a schools' booking scheme was set up well in advance of the opening, with assistance from the Manpower Services Commission. An educational package was designed by the Keeper of Archaeology, Elizabeth Hartley, who also organised participative drama sessions for school parties, with funding from the MSC and the Yorkshire Arts Association.

Placing such a major touring exhibition into our small building required a lot of work on-site, and the Museum was closed for three months at the beginning of 1982, while galleries were stripped out and heating pipes diverted, and a team of workmen built a framework of cases and corridors which included a complete thatched Viking house. The exhibition was opened on 30th March 1982 by H.R.H. The Prince of Wales, and seen by some 235,000 visitors before it closed at the end of October; however pressure on space in the Museum was such that visitor numbers had to be strictly controlled, and for much of the time there were discouragingly long queues for entry.

The Yorkshire Museum showing of this exhibition was chosen for the European Museum of the Year Special Exhibition Award, both for the presentation of the exhibition within the Museum and for the additional educational projects organised by the Keeper of Archaeology, who went to Milan for the presentation of a bronze head of the Irish poet and philosopher Aengus, donated by the Bank of Ireland.

The Viking exhibition was followed by the redevelopment of the permanent archaeological galleries, the Anglo-Saxon and Viking gallery being opened in 1983, the Roman gallery in 1985, and the St. Mary's Abbey gallery in 1988; Ivor Heal, the Viking exhibition designer, being commissioned to develop all three projects.

In 1982 both Michael Clegg and Colin Simms, the Keeper of Biology, left to devote their time to free-lance pursuits. Colin Simms was replaced by Paul Howard, previously of Inverness Museum, and early in 1983 Terence Suthers was appointed to the position of Curator.

A Lancastrian, Terry Suthers started his museum career in Hull, where he studied Roman mosaics and obtained an Open University B.A. He then moved to the Area Museum Service for Yorkshire and Humberside, first as Design and Exhibitions Officer before promotion to Deputy Director. This meant that he was already familiar with the Yorkshire Museum, as he had processed our grant applications for improved storage facilities and gallery redevelopments, and co-ordinated the practical assistance given by the Area Service to the Upper Dales Museum and the 'Vikings in England' exhibition.

Both Paul Howard and Terry Suthers proved to be very enthusiastic about the subject then under consideration for the 1984 major exhibition – dinosaurs.

I had initiated this in the summer of 1982, as a return to the Museum's own medium-sized summer exhibitions. A letter to Dr. Alan Charig of the Natural History Museum in London, one of the world's leading dinosaur experts, brought an invitation to visit the Museum in South Kensington to discuss, I hoped, the possible loan of a few items to boost our own small collection of dinosaur bones. However, when Alan Charig, his colleague Dr. Angela Milner and I started to look through their superb collection of specimens from dinosaur sites across the world, we could see the potential for a major exhibition on the subject; something which had never before been attempted in Britain.

By early 1983 the success of the 'Vikings in England' was being reflected in the improved public perception of the Museum, and when Terry Suthers and Paul Howard greeted the subject of dinosaurs with an enthusiasm which matched that of Alan Charig and Angela Milner in London, the idea of mounting a comprehensive review of the dinosaurs in York became a viable proposition. The planned redevelopment of the biology galleries was arranged so that they would be available during 1984, in addition to the geology galleries and the Central Hall, and Paul even rose to the challenge of Alan's offer of a complete *Iguanodon* skeleton – provided we dismantled it and remounted it.

By the autumn of 1983 we had put together a team with Museum, Area Service and Manpower Services Commission personnel, with Christopher Johnson-Green as the exhibition designer. The Trustees of the British Museum (Natural History) gave permission for the loan of the specimens, and allowed Alan Charig to act as Consultant; several other museums in England and Scotland also lent important specimens.

Transport of so much dinosaur material was a major undertaking, as many of the specimens were both large and extremely fragile. Several

143

members of the exhibition team spent three weeks in London packing the skulls and skeletons ready for removal, and a further week in Manchester, where the *Iguanodon* was on display – and then had to delay the scheduled transport of the specimens to York for a fortnight as fierce blizzards swept across the country in early February.

While the exhibition was being mounted, an information booklet was sent out to teachers and an advance booking system set up for school parties. Plans were also laid for a series of lectures, film shows and other linked events during the year, and a major publicity drive was undertaken.

'A New Look at the Dinosaurs' was opened in April 1984 by Professor David Bellamy, with five exhibition galleries covering every aspect of dinosaur life. In the first gallery the centre-piece was the sixteen foot high *Iguanodon* skeleton, while displays around the outside of the gallery explained the geological setting and the problems of classification of the dinosaurs. The second gallery showed, on one hand, a complete skull of the great carnivore *Tyrannosaurus*, a seven foot high arm-bone (humerus) of *Brachiosaurus* and a complete skeleton of *Massospondylus*, mounted for the exhibition by Paul Howard; and, on the other hand, a selection of unique specimens showing in graphic detail dinosaur skin, teeth, brain and nerve structure, eggs and egg-shell, a dinosaur dropping and a broken and healed *Iguanodon* leg-bone (pl. 17).

In the third gallery were displayed a selection of skulls and models illustrating the bird-hipped dinosaurs, or Ornithischia (pl. 18). Sharon Wright's glass paintings of dinosaurs in their habitat formed a feature of this gallery opposite the Dinosaur Jungle, in which living specimens of plants such as Cycads, Ginkgos, Tree-ferns and primitive conifers set the scene for a sound-track of 'dinosaur noises' created electro-acoustically by Dr. Richard Orton of York University.

The fourth gallery introduced the visitor to the history of dinosaur discovery, in Britain and elsewhere, and provided a brief résumé of dinosaur sites world-wide. The two arms of the giant Polish *Deinocheirus*, suspended from the ceiling of the gallery, were being seen in Britain for the first time. In the last gallery illustrative material was used to document the fascination which dinosaurs have for artists, film-makers and the public, and a brief explanation was given of the possible causes of their extinction. A well-stocked shop was strategically placed to attract visitors as they left the galleries.

Media interest was tremendous, with prime-time coverage on television and radio. The launch was in the same week as the opening of the York Archaeological Trust's Jorvik Viking Centre; this proved to be to our

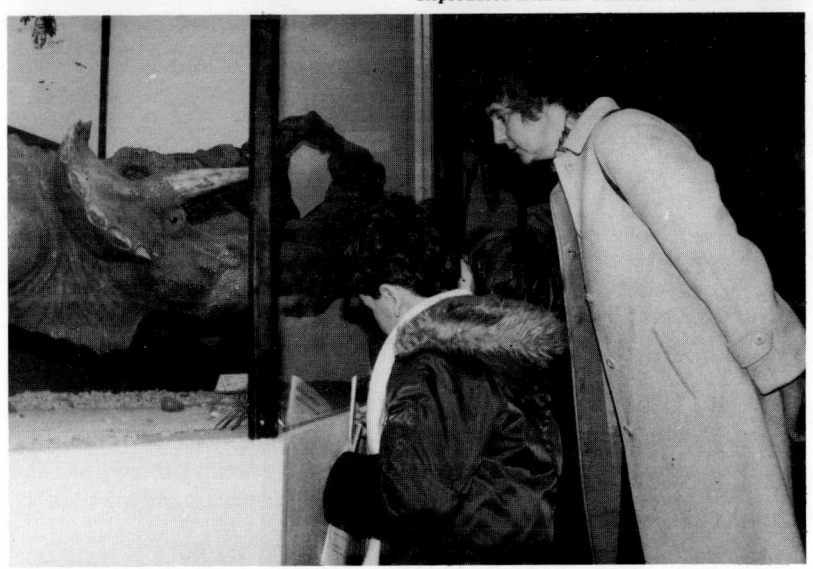

Pls. 17 & 18.   Children meet the Dinosaurs, 1984

mutual benefit as journalists took the opportunity to extend their visit to York to cover both events. To our surprise major articles on the dinosaurs in several Scandinavian publications attracted visitors from the continent to the exhibition.

International publicity was also realised when Dr. Beverley Halstead reviewed the exhibition favourably in an article for *New Scientist*; this resulted in visits from museum professionals from other countries, including Japan and the U.S.A., where major dinosaur galleries are being planned.

In addition to the programme of lectures and films, in the summer we organised a Dinosaur Gala Day in the Museum Gardens, attended by chinese-dragon style dinosaurs each propelled by up to a dozen school-children, and throughout the year we had a wide range of unsolicited models, pictures, stories and poems sent in by children, with reports by teachers of class projects based on the exhibition.

By the end of the year the dinosaurs had been seen by some 335,000 visitors, including over 43,000 pre-booked school-children. For the first time a detailed visitor survey was carried out, which showed that while 30% of the visitors came from the Yorkshire region, 20% came from London or further south. Most of the school parties were from primary schools – we were told that as dinosaurs do not fit into the secondary school curriculum they were not allowed to organise visits.

At the end of the year the specimens had to go back to London, where they are used for research by scientists from across the world, but there was no doubt that, had the exhibition remained, it would have continued to draw the crowds. Four years later, the museum office still gets enquiries about it, and a permanent dinosaur exhibition for the North of England has been discussed by more than one organisation in the area. We were able to keep the *Iguanodon* for a further year, much to the delight of local children – and of Museum staff, who were able to spread out the hard work of dismantling the various items, packing and returning them to their various homes up and down the country.

With a third of a million paying visitors the exhibition had been a financial success, and had demonstrated the potential of the Museum. As a result the County Council were able to support schemes to upgrade the facilities for visitors, with new toilets, improved heating and ventilation, and a self-contained Museum shop.

As a result of the Museum's improved image, in 1985 I.B.M. agreed to bring their computer exhibition 'Exhibit' to the Museum Gardens for its only showing in the North of England. Designed by the Italian architect

Renza Piano specifically for a city parkland setting the impressive modular 'greenhouse' housed an interactive display of the latest computer technology, and attracted over 100,000 visitors during its three-month stay in York.

In 1987 Terry Suthers left to take up the post of Assistant Director, Public Services, at the Science Museum in London, and Brian John Hayton took up the position of Curator. Born in Ayrshire in 1953 he obtained a Degree in Modern History at Glasgow University and a Diploma in Public Administration from London University. Brian started work at Glasgow Museum in 1975 as a graduate trainee and then moved to Moray Council as District Curator. He left Scotland in 1980 to take up the post of Assistant Director at the North West Museum and Art Gallery Service, was made Deputy Director the next year, and came to the Yorkshire Museum in October 1987.

Major exhibitions continue in the Museum, with 'Disappearing Forest Wildlife' in 1986 and 1987, featuring live tropical forest insects, spiders, snakes and fish, and, in 1988, 'Abbeys of Yorkshire', mounted in conjunction with English Heritage and the National Trust. Redevelopment of the public displays is continuing with the provision of new biology and geology galleries.

In 1953 George Willmot expressed the hope that, by the time of the Museums' Association's next visit to York, a new period in the history of the Museum would have dawned. The first glimmers of approaching daylight came as the Yorkshire Philosophical Society worked together with York City Council to ensure the future of the collections in York. The early sunrise was slow, obscured at times by clouds, as staff worked in the Museum basement and stores to curate the collections, a slow and painstaking task away from the public eye, but throughout the 1970's and 1980's the public and scientific standing of the Museum steadily increased, and a new era has indeed dawned for the Association's return to York for their Centennial Conference in 1988.

The imagery is indeed apt, with its cyclic implications, as in many ways the current revival of fortunes of the Museum, and of the country's museums as a whole, can be seen as a return to a previous state. Now, as in the early and mid-19th century, museums are being seen as exciting, innovative places to visit and indeed to work in; now, as then, much of the impetus for change is coming from the amateur sector, that dedicated band of people who provide invaluable and knowledgeable voluntary help to established local institutions or build up their private collections into new museums.

147

A museum exists, not just as a building or an exhibition hall or group of staff members, but as the sum of its collections and its history. As we use the collections, museum staff are constantly reminded of the debt of gratitude that we today owe to men of a century or more ago, who patiently collected, cleaned and labelled specimens so that they would survive to our day, and we are conscious that our work will be judged, not only by tomorrow's visitor, but also by Curators in the 21st and indeed 22nd centuries.

Meanwhile, if we can recapture in the Yorkshire Museum the spirit of scientific discovery that motivated its founders so long ago, and pass that enthusiasm on to our visitors, especially the children, we are repaying our debt to the past.

Appendix A

Collections of Geological Material donated to the Yorkshire Museum

The following is a list of people who have donated collections of geological material to the museum; the numerous donors of individual items are not included. Museum staff will be pleased to answer requests for further information on the geological collections, and those of natural history, archaeology, numismatics and ceramics. Basic facilities are available at the museum for research workers who wish to study the collections, and requests for loans of material, for research or for exhibition, will be considered, subject to the usual safeguards.

AFFLECK, REV., Fossil plants, 1823
AILION, MR. M., Gem stones, 1910
ALEXANDER, CAPTAIN H., Fossils, 1845
ALLIS, THOMAS, Fossils, 1824-1847
ANDERSON, DR. TEMPEST, Rocks (volcanic), 1905-1914
ANDREWS, MISS, Rocks (volcanic), 1896
ARMSTRONG, A. L., Sub-fossil egg shell fragments, 1928
ARTIS, E. T., Fossil plants, 1825
ATCHESON, H. A., Fossil bones and tusk, 1823
ATKINSON, JAMES, Fossil teeth and bones, 1823
ATKINSON, MISS, Fossils, 1828-1830
ATKINSON, MR. P., Minerals, 1825

BACKHOUSE, J., Fossil bones; minerals, 1888-1893
BACKHOUSE, J., Fossils; minerals, 1842-1847
BACKHOUSE, T., Fossils; minerals, 1823-1842
BAINES, HENRY, Fossils, 1829-1845

BARBER, MR. SHERIFF, Rocks, 1827
BARKAS, T. P., Fossil fish, 1868
BARRY, A. J., Fossil ammonites and others, 1882
BEAN, WILLIAM, Fossils, 1825-1859
BECKWITH, DR. FRANCIS, Minerals and gemstones, 1843
BELCHER, MR., Fossils, 1823
BELL, A., Fossil shells, 1919-1912
BENETT, MISS E., Fossils, 1831
BILTON, REV. W., Fossils, 1837-1838
BIRD, J., Fossils, 1823-1829
BIRLEY, MISS C., Minerals, 1893
BISHOP OF BATH AND WELLS, Fossil bones and teeth, 1826
BLAKE, REV. J. F., Fossils, 1874
BLAND, JOHN, Minerals, 1823-1829
BOLTON CASTLE MUSEUM, Fossils, 1981
BOWER, H., Fossils, 1830
BRAITHWAITE, M., Minerals, 1923
BRISTOL INSTITUTION, Fossils (casts of saurian remains), 1829-1836
BRITISH ASSOCIATION FOR THE ADVANCEMENT OF SCIENCE, Fossil bones, 1883

149

BRITISH MUSEUM (NATURAL
HISTORY), Fossils, minerals,
1848-1884
BRITISH NATURAL HISTORY SOCIETY,
Fossils, 1849-1854

CARLISLE, EARL OF, Fossils, 1823,
1828
CARNE, JOSEPH, Minerals, 1830
CAWTHORNE MUSEUM, Fossils, 1890
CHADWICK, S., Fossils, 1882-1893
CHANTREY, MR., Casts of fossil
saurians, 1823-1831
CHARLESWORTH, EDWARD, Fossils,
1845-1851
CHOLMELEY, FRANCIS, Fossils,
1824-1835
CHOLMELEY, H. P., Fossils,
1837-1855
CHOLMLEY, COLONEL, Plesiosaur,
1853
CLARKE, J. E., Fossils, 1890-1921
CLARKE, JOS (OF CINCINNATTI),
Fossils, 1842-1855
CLARKE, E., Fossils, 1881
CLAYTON, CAPT., Fossils, 1877
CLOUSTON, REV. C., Rocks, 1827
CLUTTON, W. J., Minerals, 1919
COCHRANE, MAJOR, Minerals and
marbles, 1887
COLE, CAPT. J., Fossils, 1847
COLE, VISCOUNT, Fossils, 1835
COLQUEHOUN, CAPT., Minerals, 1828
COMMELINE, REV. A. S., Rocks;
minerals, 1898
CONYBEARE, REV. W. D. (AND
MILLER, J. S.), Fossils, 1823
COOKE, P. DAVIES, Minerals, 1826
COPPERTHWAITE, MR., Fossils, 1891
COPSIE, F. J., Fossils; minerals,
1823-1843
COULHURST, REV. E., Fossils, 1826
CREYKE, JUN. (AND REV. S. CREYKE),
Fossil bones, 1823
CROFT, REV. ARCHDEACON, Fossils,
1830-1831

CROFT, REV. S., Fossils, 1829-1832
CROFT, REV. T., Fossils, 1824-1826
CROMPTON, J. S., Rocks; fossils,
1877-1878
CROMPTON, MISS H. M., Fossils;
minerals, 1877-1878
CROSS, REV. J. E., Fossils, 1891
CUMBERLAND, MR., Fossils;
minerals, 1824
CUSSONS, MISS, Minerals, 1921

DALLAS, E. W. (OF EDINBURGH),
Fossil Foraminifera, 1859
DANBY, WILLIAM, Fossils; minerals,
1823-1833
DAUBENY, PROF., Fossils, 1829
DAVY, JOHN, Rocks, 1832
DAWSON, JOSH., Fossils (plants),
1832
DEALTRY, MR., Fossils, 1824
DECK, I., Fossils and casts,
1837-1844
DENBIGH, COUNTESS OF, Fossils;
rocks, 1826-1830
DIXON, REV. W. H., Fossils; rocks,
1823
DONALDSON, SURGEON COLONEL,
Fossils, 1894-1896
DRAPER, W., Fossils, 1895
DUFFIN, E. WILLIAM, Fossils, 1830
DUNHILL, DR. C. H., Fossils;
minerals, 1883-1888
DUNN, J., Fossils, 1827-1830

EAMONSON, REV. B., Rocks; fossils,
1823-1825
EASTMEAD, REV. W., Fossils; rocks,
1823
EDEN, MISS, Fossils, 1883
EDSON, G., Fossils, 1877-1882
EGERTON, REV. T., Fossils,
1836-1847
EGERTON, SIR PHILIP DE MALPAS
GREY, Fossils and Casts,
1830-1839
ELLISON, J., Fossils; minerals,
1823-1837

ELSLEY, MISS, Fossils; minerals, 1903

ELWES, JOHN WILLIAM, Fossils, 1892

ENGEL, REV. DR. PFAFFER, Fossils, 1894-1905

ENISKILLEN, EARL OF, Fossil giant deer bones, 1840

FALCONER, DR., Fossil turtle episternum, 1844

FAWKES, HAWKSWORTH, Fossils, 1823-1830

FITZWILLIAM, EARL, Fossils, 1832-1837

FOX, G. L., Fossil giant deer, 1836

FOX, W., Fossil bones, 1873

GEOLOGICAL SURVEY, YORK OFFICE, Rocks, 1938

GEORGE, E. S., Fossil plants, 1826

GILBERTSON, WILLIAM, Fossil plants, 1833

GIBSON, JOHN, Fossil bones, 1833

GILES, U. B., Minerals; fossils, 1901

GOLDIE, GEORGE, Fossils; minerals, 1824-1826

GOSTLING, DR. WILFRED, Rocks, 1906

GOWLAND, JOHN, Fossil fish, 1837

GRAHAM, D., Fossils; rocks, 1846-1847

GRAHAM, REV. J. B., Fossils, 1826

GRAHAM, REV. JOHN, Fossils; minerals, 1823-1841

GRAVELEY, C., Fossils, 1869

GRAY, JONATHAN, Fossil ammonoids, 1835

GRAY, WILLIAM (JUNIOR), Fossils, 1827-1844

GREEN, PROF. A., Fossils, 1855

GREEN, N., Minerals, 1922

GREENWOOD, MR., Fossils; minerals, 1911

GRIESBACH, REV. A., Fossils, 1845

GUNNING, MR., Fossils; rocks, 1920

GURNEY, MISS ANNA, Fossil bones etc., 1836

GUTCH, JOHN JAMES, Fossils, 1876

HAILSTONE, SAMUEL, Fossils, 1829-1845

HALIFAX, REV. ROBERT, Fossils, 1823-1828

HAMERTON, JAMES, Fossils, 1824-1840

HARCOURT, REV. LEVESON VENABLES VERNON, Fossils; minerals, 1823-1834

HARCOURT, COL. H. V., Fossils, 1837

HARCOURT, LADY F., Fossils, 1839

HARCOURT, REV. C. VERNON, Fossils, 1824-1849

HARCOURT, REV. WILLIAM VENABLES VERNON, Fossils; minerals, 1823-1872

HARGROVE, CAPT., Fossils, 1890

HARMER, F. W., Fossils, 1919

HARRISON, PETER, Fossil Graptolites, 1881

HATFEILD, J., Fossils; rocks; minerals, 1888

HATFEILD, WILLIAM, Fossils; rocks; minerals, 1834-1844

HENSLOW, PROF., Rocks, 1823

HENWOOD, W. J., Rocks; minerals, 1829-1831

HEPWORTH, MR., Minerals and gemstones, 1823

HERRIES, SIR WILLIAM H., Fossils, 1875-1939

HEULAND, MR. H., Rocks; minerals, 1823-1826

HEY, JOHN, Fossils; casts of fishes in the Leeds Museum, 1831

HEY, REV. W. C., Fossils, 1880-1909

HIGGINS, E. T., Fossil fish and reptiles (specimens and casts), 1847-1850

HINCKS, REV. W., Fossils; minerals, 1828-1836

HIRD, H. W., Fossils; rocks, 1823
HIRD, MRS., Fossils, 1984
HORNE, W. A., Fossils, 1879, 1981
HUDLESTONE, W. H., Fossils;
  minerals, 1877-1883
HUDSON, G., Fossil fish, 1844
HUTTON, WILLIAM, Minerals,
  1828-1834

JARRETT, MRS., Fossil plants and
  bones, 1824-1825
JENKINS, REV. T., Fossils; rocks;
  minerals, 1830
JOHNSON, PROF. T., Fossils, 1916
JOHNSTONE, SIR J. V. B., Minerals,
  1827-1830

KEEPING, WALTER, Fossils; rocks,
  1880-1882
KENRICK, REV. J., Fossils,
  1845-1860
KING, T. E., Fossils, 1855
KIRBY, MR., Fossils, 1829

LADDS, C., Fossils, 1894
LAWES, J. B., Minerals, 1851
LIGHTFOOT, THOMAS, Rock cores,
  1856
LAYTON, REV. J., Fossil elephant
  teeth and bones, 1826
LECKENBY, J., Fossils, 1855-1867
LEE, DR., Fossils, 1841-1845
LEEDS, C. E., Fossil Belemnites,
  1881
LEWIS, REV. T., Fossils, 1830-1836
LISLER, J., Fossils, 1845
LLOYD, MRS., Fossils, 1879
LOSCOMBE, C., Fossils; minerals,
  1830-1832
LYELL, CHARLES, Fossils; rocks;
  minerals, 1825

MACLAUCHLAN, MR., Fossils, 1843
MANTELL, GIDEON, Fossils,
  1831-1852
MARKHAM, MISS CECILIA, Fossils,
  1825

MARSHALL, WILLIAM, Fossils;
  minerals, 1823-1857
McENERY, REV. J., Fossil bones and
  teeth, 1826
MEADE, MR., Fossil; minerals, 1824
MEYNELL, MR. T., Minerals,
  1823-1828
MEYSEY-THOMPSON, COLONEL,
  Minerals, 1920
MIDDLEMISS, C. S., Fossils; rocks,
  1881-1882
MILTON, VISCOUNT, Bones (head of
  gigantic ox), 1825-1831
MORGAN, F. C., Fossils, 1933
MORRIS, REV. F. O., Fossils;
  minerals, 1840-1844
MURCHISON, R. I. AND MRS.,
  Fossils, 1827-1831
MURRAY, DR. P., Fossils; minerals,
  1823-1849
MUSHAM, J., Fossils, 1860

NATIONAL COAL BOARD, Fossils,
  1980-1982
NECKER, PROF., Fossils, 1828-1830
NEWTON, REV. B., Fossils,
  1824-1829
NORTH EASTERN RAILWAY COMPANY,
  Fossils; rocks; meteorite
  (Middlesbrough meteorite);
  minerals, 1857-1922
NORTH, S. W., Fossils, 1881-1894
NORTHAMPTON, MARQUIS OF,
  Fossils; minerals, 1833-1846
NUNNELLY, F. C., Fossils, 1913

OOSTERHOF, W. M., Fossils, 1984

PASTORI, SIGNOR LORENZO, Rocks,
  1848
PENTON, E., Fossils, 1883
PHILLIPS, JOHN, Fossils; minerals,
  1824-1852
PHILLIPS, MISS, Fossils, 1837-1844
PICKERING, ROBERT, Fossils,
  1823-1830

PLATNAUER, H. M., Fossils;
minerals, 1883-1911
POLLARD, GEORGE, Fossil plants,
1839-1840
PRAGUE MUSEUM, Rocks; minerals,
1828
PRESTON, COOPER, Fossils,
1824-1833
PRESTWICH, JOSEPH, Fossils, 1836
PRUDHOE, LORD, Fossil plants, 1844
PUGARD, C. (OF COPENHAGEN),
Fossils, 1849

RAINE, REV. CANON, Fossils,
1877-1884
RAWSON, CHRISTOPHER, Fossils,
1831
REED, WILLIAM, Fossils, 1856-1892
RICHARDSON, CHRISTOPHER, Rocks;
minerals, 1892-1894
RICHARDSON, MR. H., Rocks;
minerals, 1901-1903
RICHARDSON, REV. H., Fossils,
1859-1860
RICHARDSON, REV. W., Fossils,
1826-1830
RICHARDSON, W., Fossils, 1845
RIPLEY, R., Fossils, 1827-1847
RIPON, DEAN OF, Minerals, 1823
ROUNDELL, R. H., Fossils, 1831
ROUNDELL, REV. DANSON
RICHARDSON, Fossils, giant
ichthyosaurus; minerals,
1857-1867

SCARBOROUGH PHILOSOPHICAL
SOCIETY, Fossil plants (casts), 1832
SCHOFIELD, REV. C. R., Minerals;
rocks, 1889
SENIOR, DR. J. R., Fossils,
1975-1980
SHARP, REV. SAMUEL, Fossils,
1823-1838
SHUTE, F., Minerals, 1887
SIMS, MR. OLLIVE, Minerals,
1827-1828
SMITH, REV. SYDNEY, Fossils, 1823

SMITH, WILLIAM, Fossils, 1824-1826
SPARSHALL, MR., Fossils, 1826
STAFFORD, MARQUESS OF, Fossils,
1826
STANHOPE, E., Fossils, 1901
STAPYLTON, STAPYLTON, Fossils;
minerals, 1828
STEPHENSON, R., Fossil fish, 1842
STOURTON, LORD, Rocks; minerals,
1823
STRANGWAYES, C. FOX, Fossils;
minerals, 1871
STRANGWAYES, MR., Fossils;
minerals, 1824
STRICKLAND, EUSTACHIUS, Fossils;
minerals, 1824-1827
STRICKLAND, SIR CHARLES, Fossils,
1909-1912
STRUVE, VON, Rocks; minerals, 1824
SUTHERLAND, DUCHESS OF, Fossils,
1834
SWAIN, MISS F. C., Fossils etc., 1869
SYKES, REV. CHRISTOPHER, Fossil
bones, 1824-1840

TASBURGH, M., Fossils, 1826
TEIGNMOUTH, LORD, Rocks;
minerals, 1887
THORPE, ANTHONY, Fossils;
minerals, 1823-1832
THORPE, FIELDEN, Fossils, inc. fine
ichthyosaur, 1880-1894
TINDALL, EDWARD, Fossils,
1857-1860
TREVALYAN, W. C., Rocks; minerals,
1829
TUKE, MR. DANIEL, Fossils;
minerals, 1823-1832
TUKE, MR. SAMUEL, Fossils and
minerals, 1823-1824
TYRCONNEL, EARL, Fossils;
minerals, 1824-1835

VERNON, CAPT. FREDERICK,
Minerals, 1823

153

VERNON, CAPT. O. V., Fossils;
rocks; minerals, 1827
VERNON, E. V., Fossils; minerals,
1826

WAINWRIGHT, MISS, Fossils;
minerals, 1896
WAKE, DR., Fossils, 1836-1838
WAKEFIELD, C., Minerals, 1918
WALFORD, REV. W., Fossils, 1825
WALKER, J. F., Fossils, 1859-1908
WALKER, REV. WILLIAM, Fossils,
1848-1849
WANKLYN, A., Fossils, 1869
WATKINS, MISS, Minerals, 1891
WEAVER, T., Fossils; rocks;
minerals, 1831-1842
WENLOCK, LORD, Fossils; minerals,
1869
WHINCOPP, W., Fossils, 1846
WHITBY MUSEUM, Fossils; minerals,
1826, 1903
WICKHAM, MISSES, Fossils,
1831-1834
WILLIAMS, REV. D., Fossils, 1837

WILLIAMS, R., Jurassic fossils, 1980
WIDDOWSON, MISS, Minerals; rocks,
1877
WILLIAMS, MAJOR, Minerals, 1891
WITHAM, HENRY M., Fossils; rocks;
minerals, 1824-1839
WOOD, EDWARD, Fossils, 1850-1880
WOOD, S. V., Fossils, 1846
WOODWARD, S., Fossils, 1825-1833
WORTLEY, JOHN, S., Fossils;
minerals, 1825
WRIGHT, J. K., Fossils, 1983
WRIGHT, WILLIAM, Fossils,
1828-1829

YORKSHIRE GEOLOGICAL AND
POLYTECHNIC SOCIETY, Fossil
bones, 1887
YORKSHIRE NATURALISTS CLUB,
Fossils, 1849-1872
YOUNG, REV. GEORGE, Fossils;
rocks, 1823-1825

ZETLAND, EARL OF, Fossil (giant
plesiosaur), 1852

154

References

ADDYMAN, P. 1981. Archaeology in York, 1831-1981. In FEINSTEIN, ed., *York 1831-1981*, York, pp. 53-87.

ALLEN, D. E. 1976. *The Naturalist in Britain*.

ANDERSON, T. & FLETT, J. S. 1902a. Preliminary report on the recent eruption of the Soufrière in St. Vincent. *Proceedings of the Royal Society of London*, 70, no. 465.

ANDERSON, T. & FLETT, J. S. 1902b. Report on the eruptions of the Soufrière in 1902, and on a visit to Montagne Pelée in Martinique. Part I. *Philosophical Transactions of the Royal Society of London*, Series A, Vol. 200, pp. 352-553, pls. 21-39.

ANDERSON, T. 1908. Report on the eruptions of the Soufrière in St. Vincent in 1902, and a visit to Montagne Pelée in Martinique. Part II, the changes in the districts and the subsequent history of the volcanoes. *Philosophical Transactions of the Royal Society of London*, Series A, Vol. 208, pp. 275-303, pls. 9-25.

ARKELL, W. J. 1927-1936. A Monograph on the British Corallian Lamellibranchia. *Palaeontographical Society (Monograph)*, pp. 1-392, pls. I-LVI.

ARKELL, W. J. 1935-1948. A Monograph on the Ammonites of the English Corallian Beds. *Palaeontographical Society (Monograph)*, pp. 1-240, pls. I-LXXVIII.

BAINES, H. 1840. *The Flora of Yorkshire*, London.

BARNET, M. C. 1972. James Atkinson – Surgeon, 1759-1839. *Annual Report of the Yorkshire Philosophical Society for 1971*, pp. 48-49.

BELL, C. R. 1970. The Swimming Bath on the Manor Shore 1837-1923. *Annual Report of the Yorkshire Philosophical Society for 1969*, pp. 33-42.

BEST, G. Evangelicism and the Victorians. In SYMONDSON, ed., *The Victorian Crisis of Faith*, London.

BIRD, C. 1881. *A short sketch of the Geology of Yorkshire*, London.

BOYLAN, P. 1972. The scientific significance of the Kirkdale Cave Hyaenas. *Annual Report of the Yorkshire Philosophical Society for 1971*, pp. 38-47.

BOYLAN, P. 1981a. A new revision of the Pleistocene mammalian fauna of Kirkdale Cave, Yorkshire. *Proceedings of the Yorkshire Geological Society*, 43.3, pp. 253-280.

BOYLAN, P. 1981b. The role of William Buckland (1784-1856) in the recognition of Glaciation in Great Britain. In NEALE & FLENLEY, eds., *The Quaternary in Britain*, London, pp. 1-8.

155

BROOKE, J. H. 1979. The natural theology of the geologists: some biological strata. In JORDANOVA & PORTER, eds., *Images of the Earth*, British Society for the History of Science, pp. 39-67.

BUCKLAND, W. 1823. *Reliquiae Diluvianae*, London.

BUCKLAND, W. 1836. *Geology and Mineralogy considered with reference to Natural Theology*, 2 vols., London.

BUTTERY, D. 1982. The Observatory rescue and restoration. *Annual Report of the Yorkshire Philosophical Society for 1981*, pp. 29-33.

CANNON, W. 1960. The problem of miracles in the 1830's. *Victorian Studies*, 4.1.

CHARLESWORTH, E. 1835a. Observations on the Crag-formation and its organic remains. *Philosophical Magazine*, 3.7, pp. 81-94.

CHARLESWORTH, E. 1835b. On the Crag of part of Essex and Suffolk. *Proceedings of the Geological Society of London*, 2, pp. 195-6.

CHARLESWORTH, E. 1845. Notice of the discovery of a large specimen of *Plesiosaurus* found at Kettleness, on the Yorkshire coast. *Annual Report of the British Association for the Advancement of Science*, 1844, pp. 49-50.

CHILTON, D. 1959. Museums and the Eighteenth Century: Scientific Instruments. *Museums Journal*, 59.2, pp. 40-44.

CLARK, J. W. & HUGHES, T. M. 1890. *The Life and Letters of Adam Sedgwick*, 2 vols., Cambridge.

CLEEVELEY, R. J. 1983. *World palaeontological collections*. (British Museum (Natural History)) London.

COCKBURN, W. 1838a. *Letter to Professor Buckland concerning the Origin of the World*, London.

COCKBURN, W. 1838b. *A Remonstrance addressed to his grace the Duke of Northumberland upon the dangers of Peripatetic Philosophy*, London.

COCKBURN, W. 1844. *The Bible defended against the British Association*, London.

COLEMAN, D. C. 1959. Museums and the Eighteenth Century: The economic background. *Museums Journal*, 59.2, pp. 38-40.

COLLINGE, W. E. 1925. John Phillips. *Annual Report of the Yorkshire Philosophical Society for 1924*, pp. 37-46.

COX, L. R. 1942. New Light on William Smith and his work. *Proceedings of the Yorkshire Geological Society*, 25, pp. 1-99.

CUVIER, G. 1812. *Recherches sur les ossemens fossiles de quadrupèdes*, 4 vols., Paris.

DALLAS, W. S. 1856. *A Natural History of the Animal Kingdom*, London.

DARWIN, C. R. 1859. *On the origin of species by means of Natural Selection*, London.

DAVIS, J. W. 1883. On the Fossil Fishes of the Carboniferous Limestone Series of Great Britian. *Scientific Transactions of the Royal Dublin Society*, Vol. I, Series II, pp. 327-600, pls. XLII-LXV.

DAVIS, J. W. 1884. On some remains of Fossil Fishes from the Yoredale Series at Leyburn in Wensleydale. *Quarterly Journal of the Geological Society of London*, 40, pp. 614-635.

DAVIS, J. 1889. History of the Yorkshire Geological and Polytechnic Society, 1837-1887. *Proceedings of the Yorkshire Geological and Polytechnic Society*, n.s. 10, pp. 1-479.

DOUGHTY, P. S. 1980. On the rocks. *Museums Association Conference Proceedings 1980*.

DOUGHTY, P. S. 1981. *The state and status of geology in United Kingdom Museums*, Geological Society of London Miscellaneous Paper No. 13.

EASTMEAD, W. 1824. *Historia Rievallensis*, London.

EDMONDS, J. M. 1975a. The Geological Lecture-courses given in Yorkshire by William Smith and John Phillips, 1824-1825. *Proceedings of the Yorkshire Geological Society*, 40.3, pp. 373-412.

EDMONDS, J. M. 1975b. The first geological lecture course at the University of London, 1831. *Annals of Science*, 32, pp. 257-275.

EDWARDS, W. 1958. The Geological Survey in Yorkshire. *Proceedings of the Yorkshire Geological Society*, 31, pp. 367-381.

EVANS, R. J. 1951. *The Headmastership of the Reverend William Johnson 1896-1915*, The Archbishop Holgate Society Special Series No. 1.

FEINSTEIN, C. 1981. Population, Occupations and Economic Development, 1831-1981. In FEINSTEIN, ed., *York 1831-1981*, York, pp. 109-159.

FOX-STRANGEWAYS, C. 1892. The Jurassic Rocks of Yorkshire. 2 vols. *Memoirs of the Geological Survey*, London.

GEE, E. A. & WILLOUGHBY, M. G. 1968. The Foundation of the Yorkshire Museum. *Annual Report of the Yorkshire Philosophical Society for 1967*, p. 25.

GEIKIE, A. 1897. *The Founders of Geology*, London.

GERNSHEIM, H. 1950. *Lewis Carroll, Photographer*, New York.

GILLISPIE, C. C. 1951. *Genesis and Geology*, Cambridge, Mass.

GORDON, A. B. 1894. *The life and correspondence of William Buckland*, London.

HALSTEAD, B. 1984. Dinosaurs are to be enjoyed. *New Scientist*, 1404, p. 28.

HARCOURT, E. W. 1880-1905. *The Harcourt Papers*, vols. 13, 14, Oxford.

HARCOURT, L. V. 1838. *The Doctrine of the Deluge*, 2 vols., London.

HARCOURT, W. V. 1861. Effects of long-continued Heat, illustrative of Geological Phaenomena. *Report of the British Association for the Advancement of Science, Thirtieth Meeting, Oxford 1860*, p. 175.

HAYWARD, J. M. 1959. Museums and the Eighteenth Century: Collectors. *Museums Journal*, 59.2, pp. 29-32.

HITCHCOCK, E. 1851. *The Religion of Geology*, London.

HOOKE, R. 1705. *The posthumous works of Robert Hooke*, London.

JOHNSON, T. 1920. The male flower or microstrobilus of *Ginkgoanthus phillipsi*. *Annual Report of the Yorkshire Philosophical Society for 1919*, pp. 1-6.

KEEPING, W. 1881. *A popular handbook to the Natural History Collection in the Museum of the Yorkshire Philosophical Society York*, York.

KENDALL, P. F. & WROOT, H. E. 1924. *Geology of Yorkshire*, 2 vols., Vienna.

KENRICK, J. 1873. A retrospect of the early history of the Yorkshire Philosophical Society. *Annual Report of the Yorkshire Philosophical Society for 1872*, pp. 34-44.

LAMARCK, J. B. 1815-1822. *Histoire naturelle des animaux sans vertèbres*, 7 vols., Paris.

LAMBRECHT, K., QUENSTEDT, W., & QUENSTEDT, A. 1938, reprinted 1978. *Palaeontologi, Catalogus bio-bibliographicus*, New York.

LISTER, M. 1684. An ingenious proposal for a new sort of maps of countreys. *Philosophical Transactions of the Royal Society of London*, 14, pp. 739-746.

LOVEJOY, O. A. 1909. The Argument for Evolution before 'The Evolution of Species'. *Popular Science Monthly*, 75, pp. 499-514, 537-549.

LYELL, C. 1838. *Elements of Geology*, London.

LYELL, C. 1839. On the relative ages of the Tertiary deposits commonly called 'Crag' in the counties of Norfolk and Suffolk. *Magazine of Natural History*, 3, pp. 313-330.

LYELL, K. M. 1881. *Life, Letters and Journals of Sir Charles Lyell*, 2 vols., London.

MARKHAM, R. 1976. Notes on Edward Charlesworth, 1813-1893. *Ipswich Geological Group Bulletin*, 18, pp. 14-16.

MATHER, K. F. & MASON, S. L. 1939, reprinted 1970. *A Source Book in Geology 1400-1900*, Harvard.

MCMILLAN, N. F. & GREENWOOD, E. F. 1972. The Beans of Scarborough; a family of Naturalists. *Journal of the Society for the Bibliography of Natural History*, 6.3, pp. 152-161.

MELMORE, S. 1930. Thomas Allis, Osteologist 1788-1875. *Annual Report of the Yorkshire Philosophical Society for 1929*, p. 3.

MELMORE, S. 1934. The glacial gravels of the Market Weighton area and related deposits. *Quarterly Journal of the Geological Society of London*, 90, pp. 141-157.

MELMORE, S. 1942-3. Letters in the possession of the Yorkshire Philosophical Society. *North Western Naturalist*, 1942, pp. 317-332, 1943, pp. 21-29, 148-160.

MELMORE, S. 1945. A catalogue of Types and Figured Specimens in the Geological Department of the Yorkshire Museum. *The North Western Naturalist*, 20.3,4, pp. 207-221, 21.1,2, pp. 72-91, 21.3,4, pp. 234-245.

MIERS, H. A. 1928. *A report on the Public Museums of the British Isles*, Dunfermline.

MORRELL, J. B. 1940. *The City of our Dreams*, London.

MORRELL, J. & THACKRAY, A. 1981. *Gentleman of Science*, Oxford.

MORRIS, J. 1845. *Catalogue of British Fossils*, London.

MORRIS, J. & LYCETT, J. 1850-1853. A Monograph of the Mollusca from the Great Oolite. *Palaeontographical Society (Monograph)*, Part I, pp. 1-130, pls. I-XV, Part II, pp. 1-147, pls. I-XV.

MUSGRAVE, C. W. 1959. Museums and the Eighteenth Century: Architecture and Art. *Museums Journal*, 59.2, pp. 35-38.

NEVINSON, J. L. 1959. Museums and the Eighteenth Century: Antiquarians. *Museums Journal*, 59.2, pp. 33-38.

ORANGE, A. D. 1972. John Phillips and the Yorkshire Philosophical Society. *Annual Report of the Yorkshire Philosophical Society for 1971*, pp. 60-61.

ORANGE, A. D. 1973. *Philosophers and Provincials: the Yorkshire Philosophical Society from 1822 to 1844*, York.

ORANGE, A. D. 1981. Science in early nineteenth-century York: The Yorkshire Philosophical Society and the British Association. In FEINSTEIN, ed., *York 1831-1981*, pp. 1-29.

OWEN, A. 1972. William Venables Vernon Harcourt, 1789-1871. *Annual Report of the Yorkshire Philosophical Society for 1971*, pp. 50-51.

158

OWEN, R. 1844. Certain belemnites preserved with a great proportion of their soft parts in the Oxford-clay of Christian-Malford, Wilts. *Philosophical Transactions of the Royal Society of London*, 134.

PEACOCK, A. J. & JOY, D. 1971. *George Hudson of York*, Clapham.

PEACOCK, A. J. 1972. Charles Wellbeloved. *Annual Report of the Yorkshire Philosophical Society for 1971*, pp. 52-53.

PEACOCK, A. J. 1981. George Leeman and Electoral Politics 1833-1880. In FEINSTEIN, ed., *York 1831-1981*, pp. 234-254.

PHILLIPS, J. 1829. *Illustrations of the Geology of Yorkshire, Part I, the Yorkshire Coast*, London.

PHILLIPS, J. 1836. *Illustrations of the Geology of Yorkshire, Part II, The Mountain Limestone District*, London.

PHILLIPS, J. 1844. *Memoir of William Smith*, London.

PLATNAUER, H. M. 1891. List of Figured Specimens in the Yorkshire Museum. *Annual Report of the Yorkshire Philosophical Society for 1890*, pp. 56-89.

PLATNAUER, H. M. 1894. Appendix to the List of Figured Specimens in the Museum of the Yorkshire Philosophical Society. *Annual Report of the Yorkshire Philosophical Society for 1893*, pp. 46-56.

POINTON, M. 1979. Geology and Landscape Painting in nineteenth century England. In JORDANOVA & PORTER, eds., *Images of the Earth*, British Society for the History of Science, pp. 84-119.

PORTER, R. 1977. *The Making of Geology*, Cambridge.

PRESTWICH, G. A. 1899. *Life and Letters of Sir Joseph Prestwich*, London.

PYRAH, B. J. 1974. Collections and Collectors of Note. 3. Yorkshire Museum. *Geological Curators Group Newsletter*, 1.2, pp. 52-55.

PYRAH, B. J. 1976-1979. Catalogue of Type and Figured Fossils in the Yorkshire Museum. *Proceedings of the Yorkshire Geological Society*, Part 1, 41.1, pp. 35-47, Part 2, 41.2, pp. 241-260, Part 3, 41.4, pp. 437-460, Part 4, 42.3, pp. 415-437.

PYRAH, B. J. 1979. Collections and Collectors of Note. 3. Yorkshire Museum. Charlesworth Catalogues. *Geological Curators Group Newsletter*, 2.4, pp. 157-172.

PYRAH, B. J. 1981. Edward Charlesworth and the British Natural History Society. 1. Material in the Yorkshire Museum. *The Geological Curator*, 3.2,3, pp. 88-92.

RAYNER, P. H. & HEMINGWAY, J. E. 1974. *The Geology and Mineral Resources of Yorkshire*, Leeds.

ROYLE, E. 1981. Religion in York 1831-1981. In FEINSTEIN, ed., *York 1831-1981*, York, pp. 205-233.

SHEPPARD, T. 1915. Bibliography of Yorkshire Geology. *Proceedings of the Yorkshire Geological Society*, 18, pp. 1-629.

SHEPPARD, T. 1918. Martin Simpson and his Geological Memoirs. *Proceedings of the Yorkshire Geological Society*, 19.4, pp. 255-344.

SHERBORN, C. D. 1940. *Where is the —— Collection?* Cambridge.

SIMMS, C. 1972. Towards a history of natural history collections at the Yorkshire Museum. *Annual Report of the Yorkshire Philosophical Society for 1971*, pp. 85-87.

159

SIMPSON, M. 1884. *The Fossils of the Yorkshire Lias*, 2nd. Ed., Whitby.

SMITH, W. *Geological Map of Yorkshire*, 4 sheets, London.

STANDING COMMISSION ON MUSEUMS AND GALLERIES 1963. *Survey of Provincial Museums and Galleries*, London.

STEARN, W. T. 1959. Museums and the Eighteenth Century: Natural History. *Museums Journal*, 59.2, pp. 44-48.

STEARN, W. T. 1981. *The Natural History Museum at South Kensington*, London.

STORM-CLARK, C. 1981. Newman, Palladio and Mrs. Beeton: The Foundation of the University of York. In FEINSTEIN, ed., *York 1831-1981*, York, pp. 285-310.

SUTHREN, R. J. 1978. Collectors and Collections of note. 15. The Tempest Anderson collection of photographs at the Yorkshire Museum. *Geological Curators Group Newsletter*, 2.2, pp. 68-77.

TATE, R. & BLAKE, J. F. 1876. *The Yorkshire Lias*, London.

TAYLOR, E. W. 1972. Recollections: The Yorkshire Philosophical Society, 1900 to 1914. *Annual Report of the Yorkshire Philosophical Society for 1971*, pp. 103-106.

THOMPSON, S. 1877. *Memorials of John Ford*, London and York.

TILLOTT, P. M. Ed. 1961. *The Victoria History of the County of York, The City of York*, pp 1-577, London.

TORRENS, H. S. 1974. Notes on some Yorkshire Museum collectors. *Geological Curators Group Newsletter*, 1.2, pp. 56-60.

TORRENS, H. S. 1975. Yorkshire Museum Collectors. *Geological Curators Group Newsletter*, 1.3, p. 153.

TORRENS, H. S., GETTY, T. A. & CRANE, M. D. 1978. Collections and collectors of note. 7. John William Elwes. *Geological Curators Group Newsletter*, 2.3, pp. 117-120.

VERNON, W. V. 1830. Further examination of the deposit of fossil bones at North Cliff in the County of York. *Philosophical Magazine*, 2.7, pp. 1-9.

VERSEY, H. C. 1975. History of Yorkshire Geology. *Proceedings of the Yorkshire Geological Society*, 40.3, pp. 335-352.

WILLMOT, G. F. 1954. The Yorkshire Museum. *Museums Journal*, pp. 143-146.

WILSON, L. G. 1972. *Charles Lyell. The years to 1841: The revolution in Geology*, Connecticut and London.

WOODWARD, H. B. 1911. *History of Geology*, London.

WRIGLEY, A. 1944. English Eocene Eulimidae with notes on the torsion of Eulima and on Charlesworth's Illustrations. *Proceedings of the Malacological Society of London*, 26 (2, 3), pp. 47-62.

YOUNG, G. 1817. *A history of Whitby*, 2 vols., Whitby.

ZITTEL, K. A. VON 1901, reprinted 1962. *History of Geology and Palaeontology*, London.

Manuscript Sources

CHARLESWORTH, E. Ms. catalogues and correspondence with William Reed are preserved in the Geology Department, Yorkshire Museum.

KNOWLES, J. A. York Artists Vol. II, a ms. scrap-book in the York Reference Library.

O'CONNOR, J. G. The origin and development of British Geological Journals. M.Sc. Thesis, Leicester.

PHILLIPS J. Ms. correspondence preserved in the Oxford University Museum includes some 60 letters from his Yorkshire Museum colleagues.

WHINCOPP, W. 'In the matter for proceedings for liquidation by arrangement or composition with creditors instituted by William Whincopp of Woodbridge in the County of Suffolk . . . taken on June 2nd 1871.' Suffolk Record Office ref. HB46:2555.

Index

Page numbers in bold type indicate biographical details about Museum personnel.

162

De la Beche, Henry, 17, 25
Dell, John Alexander, 127
Dinosaur exhibition, 143-146
Disappearing Forest Wildlife
  exhibition, 147
Dublin Museum, 59

EASTMEAD, William, 15, 17, 31
Egerton, Francis Henry, 56
Egerton, Thomas, 14
Elliot, George F., 64, 120
Elwes, John William, 100

FITTON, William Henry, 25
Ford, John, 40

GEOLOGICAL Curators' Group, 136
Geological Society of London, 10, 12,
  32, 87
Geology collections, curation, 36, 39,
  59, 85-87, 95, 98, 107, 108, 114-131,
  141, 142
Geology galleries, redisplay, 46, 48,
  59, 70, 82, 84, 93, 99, 113, 114, 118,
  119, 120, 121, 123, 129, 134
Geology, origins and early history,
  9-12
George, Edward Sanderson, 36, 39
Gibson, John, 15
Goldie, George, 24, **29**, 31, 32, 36, 38,
  44, 50, 77, 79
Grabham, Oxley, **110**, 112, 114
Graham, John, 28, 29
Graham, John Baines, 17, 28, 29, 36
Gray, Jonathan, 18

HARCOURT, Augustus John Vernon,
  20
Harcourt, Leveson Vernon, 31, 56
Harcourt, William Venables Vernon,
  2, 4, 15, 17, **18-22**, 24, 25, 28, 31,
  32, 34, 36, 40, 45, 46, 50, 56, 58, 66,
  68, 70, 72, 75, 77, 79, 84, 90, 95
Hatfeild, William Marshall, 24, **28**,
  29, 38, 40, 56
Hawes Museum, 138

Hawkins, Waterhouse, 68
Hayton, Brian John, 147
Henslow, John Stephens, 25
Hewetson, W., 50
Hinderwell, Thomas, 32
Holmes, Edith, 114
Hooke, Robert, 9
Hospitium, 41, 118, 140
Howard, Paul, 142
Hudleston, Wilfrid, 90, **91**
Hudson, George, 57, 82, 108
Hull Literary and Philosophical
  Society and Museum, 14, 16, 25, 37
Huxley, Thomas, 84

INDIAN mutiny, York meeting, 71-76
Ipswich Museum, 54

JOHNSON, William, **113**, 117

KEEPING, Walter, **104**
Kenrick, John, 4, 66, 75, 78, 82
King's Manor, 41
Kirkdale Cave, 9, 14-16, 27, 31, 33,
  87, 134

LECKENBY, John, 85
Leeds Literary and Philosophical
  Society and Museum, 14, 25, 34, 78
Lister, Martin, 9
Liverpool Museum, 85
London Geological Journal, 59-62
Lycett, John, 82, 85
Lyell, Charles, 17, 45, 53, 70, 83

MAGAZINE of Natural History, 51, 54,
  59, 84
Malton Museum, 135
Mammoth exhibition, 138
Manchester Museum, 13
Manpower Services Commission, 136,
  142, 143
Mantell, Gideon, 61
Marshall, Brown, 33
Marshall, William, *see* Hatfeild,
  William Marshall

163

Viking Kingdom of York exhibition, 136
Vikings in England exhibition, 141-142

Wagstaffe, Reginald, **120**-125
Wakefield, Charles, **81**, 89
Walker, John Francis, 2, **90**, 107, 124
Waterman, Dudley, 121
Watson, Geoffrey, 123
Watson, William, 114, 116
Wellbeloved, Charles, 4, 29, 41, 79
Westminster Review, 84
Whincopp, William, 96-99
Whitby Literary and Philosophical Society and Museum, 12, 14, 16, 25, 26, 33, 59, 135
Whytehead, W., 14
Wilkins, William, 41
Williamson, John, 33
Willmot, George Francis, 5, 118, 124, **125**-129, 133
Wilson, Thomas, 78
Wood, Edward, 99
Wood, Searles, 53
Woodward, Samuel Pickworth, 84
Wrangham, Archdeacon, 32
Wrigley, Arthur, 64

York Academic Trust, 122
York and District Field Naturalists' Society, 80, 108
York Archaeological Society, 79
York Archaeological Trust, 135, 140, 141
York Corporation, 130, 134
York Exhibition, 1866, 88

York Literary and Philosophical Society, 13
York School of Design, 60
Yorkshire Agricultural Society, 78
Yorkshire Aircraft Museum, 135
Yorkshire and Humberside Collections Research Unit, 136
Yorkshire Antiquarian Club, 63, 79
Yorkshire Architectural and York Archaeological Society, 79
Yorkshire Geological Museum (proposed), 128
Yorkshire Geological and Polytechnic Society, 12, 77-79, 128
  museum, 78
Yorkshire Museum, additions to building, 82-87, 112
  acquisition of Museum Gardens site, 41
  bombed, 1942, 120-121
  first premises (Low Ousegate), 27
  foundation meeting, 22
  official opening 1830, 41
  ownership passed to York Corporation, 130
  ownership passed to North Yorkshire County Council, 135
  repairs, 134
Yorkshire Museum of Farming, 135, 138
Yorkshire Naturalists Club, 63, 79, 84
Yorkshire Philosophical Society, foundation meeting, 22
Young, George, 15, 31, **33**, 40, 85

Zoological Record, 84, 87
Zoological Society of London, 47